Essential
Food & Drink
ITALY

by

SUSAN CONTE

Susan Conte studied domestic science and taught cookery before marrying her Italian husband. She has lived and travelled extensively in Italy for over 20 years and has a broad knowledge of and great enthusiasm for Italian cuisine. She is the author of a book on authentic pasta and pizzas.

Produced by the Publishing Division of
The Automobile Association

Written by Susan Conte
Consultant: Bridget Jones
Copy Editors: Barbara Croxford,
Audrey Horne

Edited, designed and produced by
AA Publishing. Map © The
Automobile Association 1992.

Distributed in the United Kingdom
by AA Publishing, Fanum House,
Basingstoke, Hampshire, RG21 2EA.

A CIP catalogue record for this
book is available from the British
Library.

ISBN 0 7495 0437 4

Published by The Automobile
Association.

Typesetting: Avonset, Midsomer
Norton, Bath
Colour separation: Scantrans P.T.E.,
Singapore
Printed in Italy by Printers SRL,
Trento

*Front cover picture: Melanzane alla
parmigiana*

This book employs a
simple rating system for
dishes and specialities
in the A–Z sections on
foods and drinks:

♦♦♦   something really
         special

♦♦   try it if you can

♦   worth a try if you
         come across it

ABOUT THIS BOOK

One of the pleasures of travelling is sampling the local food and drink. Whether your tastes are adventurous or conservative, this book will whet your appetite and give you a genuine taste of Italy. It is the perfect companion to any meal, and may even change your ideas about what's on offer – it's not all pizza and pasta!

Not only will this book help you to appreciate the true flavours of the country, the practical information will enable you to cope with new or unfamiliar situations, taking the worry out of getting what you want.

Italy's regions are colourfully described, with the emphasis on local foods and specialities, and a look at the influences and traditions that you can still detect in them.

A comprehensive A–Z covers the foods you are likely to see in shops and markets and the dishes that appear on menus, with star ratings to help you make choices. Where items in this list are mentioned elsewhere in the text they are printed in small capitals, thus: GNOCCHI. There is advice on some of the best wines and the more unassuming ones worth sampling, and an A–Z of other drinks, both alcoholic and non-alcoholic, also star rated.

The guide to shopping describes the different types of establishments and what services they offer, what you can buy and when it is in season. There are useful phrases and lists of groceries with simple phonetics. The recipes include some of the most famous regional dishes and will appeal to cooks of all abilities.

A short section highlights the types of food and dishes eaten on high days and holidays and advises on what is seasonally available.

Trying to understand the menu can sometimes be a nightmare. The **Eating Out** section gives advice and phrases to use in a variety of establishments, as well as hints on how to order drinks. There are also tips on catering for babies and children, special diets and coping with a tight budget.

To round off there are more phrases, with a pronunciation guide and conversion tables to help with shopping and cooking.

INTRODUCTION

Unless you have visited Italy or been fortunate enough to find a good Italian restaurant where you live, Italian food may mean no more to you than spaghetti, tomato sauce, pizza and ice-cream. The dishes you will meet on an Italian trip, or in the pages of this guidebook, however, will, hopefully, arouse your enthusiasm for this varied, adaptable and deliciously colourful Mediterranean cuisine!

There is plenty for all tastes just waiting to be accompanied by the local red or white wine or cool, sparkling mineral water. Starters range from the rustic freshly sliced Parma ham served on hot crunchy garlic bread to the more sophisticated chilled seafood salad packed with prawns, clams, mussels, octopus and squid served in a crisp celery salad.

The pasta and rice combinations are never ending. Apart from the well-known tomato sauce and lasagne, you can find vegetable, fish and meat sauces to suit every occasion – a real treat for the tastebuds. Try the different pasta shapes mixed with aubergines, peppers or courgettes. Taste the cream sauces mixed

Tagliatelle-maker at work. You can make pasta yourself, but it is less easy than it looks

INTRODUCTION

The best place to buy fruit and vegetables is a market stall, with everything fresh and in season

with smoked salmon or prawns or crumbled sausage meat or wild mushrooms, peas and diced ham. Do not miss the bean soups, the polenta or the savoury rice risottos.

If you still have room, the excellent meat, fish and cheese dishes are waiting to tempt you. The delicately flavoured escalopes, barbecued spring lamb, roast cheeses or a freshly caught fish baked in the oven with herbs and spices take a lot of beating.

The fresh vegetables of course, whether sautéed in oil and garlic, tossed in melted butter or dressed with deliciously fragrant olive oil and freshly squeezed lemon juice, just cannot be missed. A temptingly colourful display can often be seen in the restaurants.

The dessert course varies from season to season with mountains of fresh fruit always available: juicy oranges, mandarins and kiwi fruit in the winter, succulent cherries, peaches, apricots and melons in the summer, not forgetting the luscious fresh figs and black and white grapes in all shapes and sizes. Mouthwatering sweets and local cheeses complete the feast, which must be followed by a cup of the Italian national drink: richly roasted black coffee . . . and perhaps just a thimbleful of what the Italians call a *'digestivo'*.

Buon appetito!

THE REGIONS OF ITALY

Italy's long narrow peninsula, over 1,500km (930 miles) from top to toe, with its high mountain ranges of the Alps (Alpi), Dolomites (Dolomiti) and Apennines (Appennini), enjoys a relatively sheltered position in the middle of the Mediterranean sea. However, the climate varies enormously from north to south and between mountain, plain and coast. This, together with a history of invasions and the fact that, before the Unity of Italy in 1861, each of the individual states had its own identity, customs and cuisine, has greatly influenced Italian food. The Alpine regions are known for game and POLENTA (a type of maize porridge); the sub-Alpine parts for rice and meats; the northern valleys and plains for stuffed pastas, salami, cheeses, cream and butter; the Apennines for spicy pastoral dishes; the centre and south for olive oil and pasta; and the deep south, with its hot sun, for fruit, ripe, red tomatoes and peppers, and aubergines. Excellent fish soups and seafood around the coasts complete the picture. Common to all regions are the staples of dried beans and salted cod. Whatever the dish, there is one vital element in all good Italian cooking: the use of fresh vegetables.

Piedmont and Valle d'Aosta

The beautiful mountain region of Valle d'Aosta nestles in the shadow of Mont Blanc. The crystal-clear lakes and mountain torrents are full of trout, and many different types of game can be found in the woods and forests. The lower Alpine pastures provide succulent grazing for cattle, the grasses giving the local milk and cheese their excellent flavour.

The winters, however, are very hard here, and the food must be both warming and nourishing. The first courses are mainly soups full of bread or barley, while GNOCCHI and rice served with FONTINA cheese and butter can be found all year round. FONTINA is also used to make FONDUTA ALLA VALDOSTANA, served sprinkled with slivers of truffle from neighbouring Piedmont (Piemonte). Traditionally, game, such as deer, hare and partridge, is prepared *in civet* or *in salmi* and marinated with herbs and spices for at least two days before being cooked. The salting of meat is a very old tradition, still found in certain regions; look out for the CARBONADE in the smaller *trattorie* along the valleys. One traditional dish, still easily found today is TROTA SPACCATA (spiced fried trout).

To finish the meal, especially when it is snowing outside, why not try a CAFFÈ VALDOSTANO (Valle d'Aosta-style coffee)?

Piedmont, to the south of Valle d'Aosta, gets excellent olive oil from Liguria to make one of its most traditional dishes, the savoury dip known as BAGNA CAÖDA. Contrasting with this simple concoction are the dishes handed down from the

THE REGIONS OF ITALY

noble families of the court of Savoy. In the cafés in Turin (Torino) you can still see traces of this past opulence in the baroque mirrors and the crystal vases full of tempting *gianduiotti*, hazelnut-flavoured chocolates wrapped in gold paper. Turin could be considered the home of Italian chocolate as it was brought here in the 18th century from France. CIOCCOLATA CALDA is a must, and so are the cakes and pastries.

Before lunch, treat yourselves to an *aperitivo* – Vermouth was invented in Piedmont. Starters come in the form of salads made with slivers of raw meat (CARPACCIO), truffle-flavoured mushrooms, the famous BAGNA CAÖDA dip or a creamy FONDUTA from the neighbouring Valle d'Aosta. After this rich beginning, you can continue with meat-filled *agnulot* (ravioli) or a winey RISOTTO AL BAROLO or, when the weather is cool, a PANISCIA (thick soup) or a bowl of BRODO (consommé). The Piedmontese prefer to serve their pasta *in brodo* rather than with a sauce. Alba is famous for its TARTUFO BIANCO. Here the restaurants serve their first courses, and most of their main courses, topped with slivers of this unusual strong-tasting 'white' truffle. Meat dishes such as BRASATO AL BAROLO (marinated, braised beef), or game cooked with red wine and mushrooms, are two of the richer main courses, along with FRITTO MISTO (mixed fry), which often includes frogs' legs, cubes of sweet semolina and tiny

9

ITALY

0   100   200 km
0   50   100 miles

AUSTRIA

HUNGARY

Trentino-Alto Adige
Bolzano
Dolomiti
Trento
Friuli-Venezia Giulia
Udine
Lago di Garda
Veneto
Vicenza
Treviso
Trieste
Verona
Padova
Mantova
Venézia
Po
Ferrara
Golfo di Venézia
Módena
Comácchio
Romagna
Ravenna
Bologna
YUGOSLAVIA
Prato
Forlì
Rimini
SAN MARINO
Firenze
Ancona
Arezzo
Toscana
Marche
L. Trasimeno
Grosseto
Perúgia
San Benedetto
Umbria
Ascoli Piceno
2914m
Viterbo
Terni
Pescara
L'Aquila
Abruzzo
Lazio
Molise
ROMA
Latina
Cassino
Foggia
Benevento
Barletta
Campania
Bari
Napoli
Potenza
Puglia
Salerno
Brindisi
Golfo di Salerno
Táranto
Lecce
Basilicata
Golfo di Táranto
Rossano
Calabria
Cosenza
Crotone
Isole Eólie o Lipari
Catanzaro
Palermo
Messina
Trápani
Réggio di Calábria
C. Spartivento
Marsala
Etna 3323m
Caltanissetta
Catania
Agrigento
Sicilia
Isole di Pantelleria
Ragusa
Siracusa
C.Pássero

almond macaroons. As all the ingredients are dipped in batter you cannot tell which is which until you bite into them! Other typical main courses are BOLLITO MISTO IN SALSA VERDE (mixed meats in a green sauce), and trout grilled over a wood fire. A popular summer dish is VITELLO TONNATO (cold veal with tuna mayonnaise) whose origin is contended between Piedmont and Lombardy.

If you can still find a place for a little cheese, try TOMINI or BROSS. The latter, however, is only for lovers of strong flavours! In the country shops and *trattorie* you can find an excellent selection of local salami, buried in lard or in earthenware jars, or salted shoulder of pork.

GRISSINI, Italy's world famous bread sticks, first made in Turin in the 17th century, are now an important industry. However, homemade ones of different widths, lengths and flavours can still be found in bakers' shops.

Lombardy

The Lombards are known for being hard workers and not having much time to spend in the kitchen; Lombardy (Lombardia) was the first region to make one-course meals by serving its RISOTTO ALLA MILANESE with OSSOBUCO. Traditional cookery books, however, contain dishes ranging from the quickly prepared ZUPPA PAVESE (consommé with eggs) to the elaborate CASSOEULA (pork and cabbage casserole) and the

famous Christmas bread PANETTONE, taking a whole day to make.

Bergamo and Bréscia serve a lot of POLENTA, either with STRACOTTO (tender cooked beef) or small game birds from the neighbouring valleys. The cattle on the Padua plain not only provide meat for braised and boiled stews but also the excellent dairy produce exported all over the world. Famous cheeses such as GRANA, GORGONZOLA and TALEGGIO are produced, along with the creamy ROBIOLA, STRACCHINO and MASCARPONE (more like a thick clotted cream). The local GRANA (hard cheese) is *parmigiano-lodigiano* which, they say, is even richer than the world-famous Parmesan cheese, *parmigiano-reggiano*. The ancient town of Mantua (Mantova) is famous for its TORTELLI DI ZUCCA and RISOTTO ALLA MANTOVANA or *alla pilota* (with salami and Parmesan), whereas Cremona makes *torrone* (honey and almond nougat) and MOSTARDA (fruit pickled in mustard sauce). Across the Padua plain, near Pavia, along the banks of the rivers Ticino and Po, you can find restaurants offering frogs' legs served on a bed of risotto or eels cooked in butter, onions, wine and nutmeg. Dishes of freshwater fish are also found at the lakeside *trattorie* around Lake Como which specialise in *risotto con pesce persico* and MISSULTITT (made from salted, dried fish). In the nearby Valtellina valley, the famous PIZZOCCHERI (ribbon pasta) is still served layered with the local BITTO cheese, and BRESAOLA (dried fillet of beef) is served both as a starter and cooked with onions, mushrooms and spices to make *concia*.

All over Lombardy one common denominator prevails in cooking, and that is butter. It was first used for dressing vegetables by Valerio Leonte, a Milanese nobleman, who served *asparagi al burro* to Julius Caesar on his return from Gaul, and it has since been used to dress or sauté vegetables all over the north. Butter is also used to fry COSTOLETTA ALLA MILANESE, the veal cutlet which has become a national favourite. The finely minced *luganica* sausage has also found its way all over Italy.

Trentino–Alto Adige

The Dolomites mountain range dominates this area of Italy. Dishes such as *polenta carbonera*, made from POLENTA mixed with salami, onions, a strong-flavoured local cheese and 50 grams (2oz) of butter per head, will give you an idea of the type of food to expect – both nourishing and warming. This, together with the rich sauces to accompany game and POLENTA, form the basis of traditional Trentino cooking. Unfortunately, in the tourist season national and international dishes tend to be served in preference to local food. However, one local dish worth seeking out is the sweet-sour *vitello alle mele renette*, a wonderful combination of

Lake Orta: break for refreshment

apples and highly spiced meat. Trentino–Alto Adige is the main apple producing region in Italy, exporting fruit to many parts of the world.

The mild basin around Lake (Lago di) Garda produces citrus fruits and olive oil for summer salads. However, when winter arrives, back comes POLENTA, served with rich sauces made from the wild mushrooms which abound in August and September. Trentino has over 300 lakes, and freshwater fish, such as trout, are on most menus.

In Alto Adige, to the north of Trento, you immediately feel

the Austrian influence. German is spoken everywhere, pasta no longer appears on menus, and in its place you find CANEDERLI (smoked ham and sausage dumplings) served in consommé or, like the occasional ravioli, coated in melted butter and Parmesan cheese. Pork, *pancetta* (bacon), WURSTEL (frankfurters) or the smoked SPECK (ham), play a large part in the local cuisine. STINCO DI MAIALE AL FORNO, with its crisp, crunchy, crackling, can be found on most menus, served with boiled or fried potatoes, POLENTA or *crauti* (sauerkraut); and beer is often preferred to wine. Steaks are also served with a spicy onion sauce or coated with cream and mushrooms, Austrian style. The cake shops reflect the Austrian influence, too, with their chocolate *sachertorte*, fresh fruit tarts with wild strawberries, raspberries and bilberries, and, of course, STRUDEL with apples, nuts and cinammon.

Veneto

This region, surrounding Venice (Venézia) and its lagoon and stretching inland to the foothills of the Dolomites, has survived on a staple diet of POLENTA since the 16th century, when the maize used to make it was first brought to Italy by the Venetian traders. *Risi (riso*, rice, written in the plural) is peculiar to Veneto where it is cooked to be neither too solid nor too liquid, but *all'onda* – which means it will ripple or 'make waves'. This type of rice, cooked with vegetables, salami, meat, fish or seafood is served as a first course, RISI E BISI being one of the better known dishes. Pasta is used in soups such as *pasta e fas oi* (PASTA E FAGIOLI). Veneto is also famous for its poultry, fish and offal. FEGATO ALLA VENEZIANA (calves' liver with onion) has become a dish that is popular from Venice down to Sicily. *Bacalà* is served frequently. This is not salted cod (*baccalà*), but dried cod, or STOCCAFISSO. BACALÀ MANTECATO (dried cod whisked with garlic and olive oil) is one of the most popular ways of serving it, with POLENTA, of course! The Adriatic Sea and the Venetian Lagoon supply Venice and Veneto with fish of all shapes and sizes. These are grilled, baked, fried, stuffed or poached, or made into *brodeto*, the local fish soup. Sardines and sole are marìnated in SAOR, a spicy sauce once used to camouflage the taste of fish that was neither too fresh nor of good quality. Going inland again towards Treviso, poultry in the form of chicken, duck, pigeon, goose, turkey and guinea fowl is served with strongly-flavoured PEVERADA sauce. Treviso is also famous for its RADICCHIO (red-leaved chicory) served as a salad or grilled over a wood/charcoal fire. Veneto is not without its famous cakes. The Christmas PANDORO comes from Verona, the home

Veneto's lush wine country

of Romeo and Juliet. For anyone who does not have a sweet tooth, bars down Venice's narrow *calli* offer titbits of hard-boiled eggs and tiny crabs to accompany the local wines.

Friuli–Venezia Giulia

Although famous for its wines, this small region tucked away between Veneto, Austria and Yugoslavia, is not so well known for its food. Foreign influence (Trieste was one of the main ports during the Austrian-Hungarian empire) accounts for the many sweet and sour dishes and savoury food flavoured with cinnamon and sugar, like CIALZONS FRIULANI or CIALZONS ALLA CARNIA (stuffed pasta squares). This unusual sweet and sour combination can also be found in the GNOCCHI served in Trieste which have a plum hidden in their middle.

Apart from these pasta dishes, the people of Friuli enjoy traditional soups made from potatoes, barley, beans and pumpkin, such as JOTA, and POLENTA dishes. Friuli has its own sauerkraut called *brovade*, traditionally served with *muset*, a boiled, spiced sausage.

In Carnia, the mountainous region, the characteristic *trattorie* offer regional dishes, some of which originate from Slavic cuisine. They also make FRITTATA CON ERBE (herb omelette), packed with whatever herbs happen to be in season. Half way between the mountains and the coast is San Daniele, the town which gives its name to one of the best cured hams in Italy. It is sweeter than the one from Parma and ideal for serving with melon as a starter. Down on the coast look for fish risottos and the local *brodeto* (fish soup). Dressed crab (*granseola*) is also a speciality. Cakes and pastries also reflect a foreign influence; GUBANA (sweet bread roll) is of Slavic origin, for example.

Liguria

Although Liguria, on the Ligurian Sea in the northwest, is mountainous, allotments abound as the climate is excellent. The local cuisine is therefore based on vegetables and herbs as well as fish. The coast is full of olive groves. The olive oil is so light that it is often enjoyed sprinkled on

Cultivating vegetables in Liguria

FOCACCIA (bread-like pizza), with just a little sea salt, to make a delicious snack. It is also used to make a soup called MESCIUÀ (bean, sweetcorn and chick-pea soup).

The Ligurians make savoury cakes and stuffed pizzas, such as TORTA PASQUALINA, served at Eastertime. And it is not surprising that PESTO is one of the best known sauces, since basil, which has a particular flavour in Liguria, grows everywhere. It sprouts out of old tin cans on balconies and from terracotta vases on windowsills, as well as being found in gardens and allotments.

Fish is cooked and served in all possible ways. BURIDDA (fish and vegetable stew) and CIUPPIN are both typical fish dishes, and STOCCAFISSO (dried cod), which was the staple diet aboard ship, is cooked in an earthenware casserole with olives, potatoes and pine kernels. The real Ligurian fish masterpiece, however, is CAPPON MAGRO which must be the richest *maigre* dish (for a fast, or day of fasting), in all the cuisine of Italy!

Meat does not play a large part in the Ligurian kitchen. The most characteristic meat dish is CIMA RIPIENA (stuffed veal), with more filling than meat. Eggs, cheese and vegetables are also used to stuff the local RAVIOLI. In Genoa (Genova), visit the *friggitorie* where almost anything is fried in the local olive oil. In the antique-looking cake shops you can sample local specialities made from cocoa, candied peel and almond paste. *Pan dolce*, the Ligurian Christmas cake, is full of pine kernels, pistachio nuts, candied peel and raisins.

Emilia–Romagna

TORTELLINI (ring-shaped pasta), smothered in cream and cheese, characterise Emilia–Romagna, in north central Italy, where they certainly live to eat and not eat to live! Home-made *pasta all'uovo* (egg pasta) is cut into *tagliatelle* or used to make stuffed pasta, which changes its name according to the filling or place of origin. *Cappelletti* (little pasta hats) are made in Romagna, where one of the filling ingredients is the local *raviggiolo* cheese, whereas in Ferrara they are stuffed with minced brains and turkey breast. Modena is famous for its square-shaped RAVIOLI filled with minced roast meats, while Bologna is the place to find the famous TORTELLINI which, legend has it, were modelled on Venus' navel! *Tortelli* in Piacenza and Parma are filled with RICOTTA cheese and spinach, while in Ferrara they are called *cappellacci* and stuffed with pumpkin and cheese. The main ingredient in classic lasagne is the rich, meaty BOLOGNESE sauce. Emilia is also famous for its cured hams and dried sausages or INSACCATI (meaning 'put in a bag'), like salami, or the pear-shaped *culatello* from Parma, so highly prized that the Marquis of Pallavicini was

known to have given them as wedding gifts! Parma is of course better known for its ham, *prosciutto di Parma*, while Modena produces the famous ZAMPONE (a spiced sausage) and MORTADELLA, the luncheon meat which is delicious eaten in a PIADINA ROMAGNOLA (soft, flat bread eaten filled and folded), heated on a griddle at the roadside. *Salama da sugo* (local salami) was served as an aphrodisiac by the ruling Este family and even today can be found at wedding banquets! The local cheese is, of course, *parmigiano-reggiano* (see GRANA), the world-famous Parmesan which is generously sprinkled over everything except the fish from the Adriatic coast. Again we find the local BRODETTO (this time spelt with two ts) and also seasoned fish coated in breadcrumbs and cooked on the spit, or eels from Comácchio. Rich sweet dishes such as ZUPPA INGLESE (a sort of trifle), or *pan pepato* from Ferrara, a sweet bread crammed with almonds, walnuts and pine kernels, complete the meal.

Tuscany

The rolling hills of Tuscany (Toscana), with their green and brown patchwork and gnarled olive trees, are redolent of an Italian way of life which is reflected in the simple, wholesome local cuisine: the famous BISTECCA ALLA FIORENTINA (or just *fiorentina*) – a thick steak grilled over a wood or charcoal fire – being

Family lunch in a Lucca restaurant

an excellent example. During the Renaissance Florentine nobles ate lavishly. Ordinary people, however, ate very simply. The most common 'filler' at that time was CASTAGNACCIO, made from chestnut flour and now eaten as a cake. Crusty bread sprinkled with the magnificent Tuscan olive oil with its full, intense flavour was also, and still is, a favourite filler.

Pasta is sometimes eaten in the form of PAPPARDELLE AL SUGO DI LEPRE (ribbon pasta with a hare sauce), but more typical first courses are vegetable soups, thick ones such as RIBOLLITA or thin ones like ACQUA COTTA, which is served in the Tuscan Maremma near Grosseto. Grilled meats of all kinds have pride of place on menus. Beef, lamb, pork, poultry and game are barbecued over a wood or charcoal fire or roasted in the oven, as with the pork dish ARISTA DI MAIALE. Another

favourite main course is grilled pigs' liver flavoured with bay leaves. Chicken livers are minced and served on toast as CROSTINI.

Famous cured meats, like the salamis FINOCCHIONA and SOPPRESSATA, are made from pork, but down in the Maremma you can find hams and sausages made from wild boar (CINGHIALE).

Fish dishes such as CACCIUCCO, a fish soup, or TRIGLIE ALLA LIVORNESE (red mullet cooked with chillies), can be found all along the coast, and near Pisa they also specialise in eels cooked with garlic and sage.

Beans are probably the most characteristic vegetable, as Tuscan beans are very versatile. Haricot beans were originally cooked in a Chianti flask. FAGIOLI AL FIASCO can still be found on menus along with FAGIOLI ALL' UCCELLETTO, cooked with tomato and sage. The delicious local cheeses, made from ewes' milk, can be bought direct from farms or stalls in markets or at local *feste*. Here you can also find *brigidini*, little aniseed cakes cooked on a griddle at the stall.

Most Tuscan restaurants will offer CANTUCCI biscuits and a glass of the sweet Vin Santo to complete your meal, but in Siena you may be offered the local PANFORTE (Christmas cake) or RICCIARELLI (small marzipan cakes) instead.

Umbria

This small central region, with its medieval towns of Assisi, Gubbio and Perúgia, offers good, wholesome cooking and delicious grilled meats, very similar to Tuscany's. The olive oil is excellent, though not produced on a large scale, but the 'star' ingredient of Umbrian cuisine is the TARTUFO NERO (black truffle). At weekends, during the summer months, Umbrian villages and towns hold *sagre* (festivals) to venerate the truffle. Black truffle is added in handfuls to sauces, chopped into a paste with anchovies and spread on toast to make *crostini neri*. It is also served with *stringozzi*, a home-made pasta from Spoleto made from flour and water, and added to omelettes and the cheesey bread called PIZZA DI PASQUA. The wild ASPARAGI (asparagus) found in the countryside are made into a cream sauce and served with pasta, added to risottos or served as a vegetable. When in season, they are often an excuse for another *sagra*. Norcia is famous for its pork and pork products such as SALSICCE (sausages), *finocchiella* (fennel-flavoured salami), LONZA (a lean salami) and MEZZAFEGATO an unusual-tasting pigs' liver sausage. In Rome you can even find shops called *Norcineria* which sell pork, ham and salami. Game-lovers can find wild doves and small birds roasted on the spit with a sauce called *alla GHIOTTA* (or *leccarda*). Another traditional way of cooking chicken, duck or rabbit is IN PORCHETTA.

Even though Umbria has no coastline, you can get fish from the lakes of Trasimeno and Piediluco; and the trout of the Fonti del Clitunno (between Spoleto and Assisi) are just waiting to jump on your line, the lakes are so full!

Biscuits for dipping in wine are again popular, along with cakes made from almonds, glacé cherries and nuts. The most unusual cakes are *stinchetti*, tiny marzipan replicas of human tibias (leg bones) which, when eaten, are supposed to fortify and protect the bones!

The Marches

The largest wholesale fish market on the Adriatic coast is in San Benedetto, so fish is obviously one of the main regional foods. The BRODETTO DI PESCE served from Pesaro down to Ancona is made from thirteen varieties of fish cooked in tomato sauce (the superstitious are allowed to add one or two more!), whereas the fish soup from Porto Recanati down to San Benedetto is flavoured with saffron and has no tomatoes. STOCCAFISSO (dried cod) pops up yet again and is cooked with tomatoes and potatoes (called *in potacchio*) which turn it into a real delicacy.

Inland, the traditional first course is VINCISGRASSI, similar to lasagne. The name, legend says, comes from the distorted local pronunciation of Prince 'Windisch-Graetz', a captain in the Austrian army fighting against Napoleon, who apparently tasted this dish while in Ancona. Stuffed pasta is found in Pesaro where *cappelletti in brodo* is a favourite, especially at Christmas time. Home-made *tagliatelle* is served with a rich RAGÙ and generously sprinkled with grated PECORINO cheese. Near Pesaro you can find RAVIOLI stuffed with ricotta cheese and served, rather unusually, with a fish sauce.

The local olives are large and fleshy, and perfect for turning into OLIVE ASCOLANE (stuffed, fried green olives), which are an essential ingredient in the local FRITTO MISTO ALL'ITALIANA.

Rome and Latium

The typical Roman *osteria* (inn) has its own special character in its décor of plain, painted walls and its wooden tables covered with fresh sheets of paper. It is in these family-run businesses that you can sample the real Roman cooking known as *casalinga* or *casareccia*: unpretentious, plain, home cooking, prepared with first-class local ingredients from the fertile countryside of Latium (Lazio). The traditional pasta dishes such as homemade *fettuccine con ragù*, *rigatoni alla pagliata* (ribbed pasta with calves' intestines in a tomato sauce), *spaghetti alla carbonara* and *bucatini all'amatriciana* (thick spaghetti pasta with a tomato and chilli sauce) are all served smothered in grated *pecorino* cheese. The thick pasta and pulse soups such as PASTA E FAGIOLI (with beans), PASTA E LENTICCHIE (with lentils) and PASTA E CECI (with chick-peas) can be found on all *osteria* menus along with the lighter STRACCIATELLA (broth with egg and cheese).

The main courses can be divided into two categories: the more 'sophisticated' lamb dishes, such as ABBACCHIO ARROSTO (roast lamb) and ABBACCHIO ALLA SCOTTADITO (grilled chops) with INVOLTINI DI MANZO (beef rolls) and SALTIMBOCCA ALLA ROMANA (veal escalopes flavoured with ham and sage); and the more down-to-earth offal dishes such as CODA ALLA VACCINARA (oxtail stew), TRIPPA ALLA ROMANA (tripe in a tomato sauce) or the unique PAGLIATA, made from the milk-filled intestines of a suckling calf.

The vegetables are many and varied: broccoli, CICORIA and BROCCOLETTI (the last two being leafy vegetables which can be bitter) are usually sautéed in olive oil with garlic and sometimes chillies. These, with CARCIOFI ALLA ROMANA (artichokes stuffed with garlic and herbs), when in season, are among the most typical. On Sundays, the Romans often go to the country for lunch where a starter of BRUSCHETTA (garlic toast) served with slices of LONZA (a kind of ham or salami) might precede the pasta; or they may pick up some PORCHETTA (stuffed roast pork) from a roadside stall to take on a picnic. Back in Rome, we must not forget the pizzerias, usually crowded on Sunday evenings, serving PIZZA, SUPPLÌ (fried rice balls) and CROSTINI (savoury toast). Roman pizzas are definitely on a par with those served in Naples, though they are thinner and more biscuity. The bars offer a variety of *tramezzini* (sandwiches) difficult to equal in other parts of Italy, and their MARITOZZI CON LA PANNA (sweet cream-filled buns) make a perfect mid-morning snack.

Abruzzo and Molise

This mountainous area, which climbs up to Gran Sasso, the highest peak in the Apennines, is a region of sheep farmers. The main course is nearly always lamb, mutton or goat, served grilled, roasted, casseroled, stewed or coated in egg and breadcrumbs and fried. *Agnello arrosto* (roast lamb), *agnello all'arrabbiata* (lamb with tomatoes and chillies) or *agnello cacio e uova* (with egg and cheese) are a few favourites. CAPRETTO (baby goat) is barbecued on

Feast your eyes in a Roman market

the spit or baked in the oven, while the entrails of both lamb and goat are cooked in seasoned tomato sauce and wine. Whole young pigs are roasted to make PORCHETTA. The cheaper offcuts are marinated in a vinegar mixture, then casseroled with chilli to make the famous *'ndocca 'ndocca* from Teramo. PEPERONCINO (chillies) are again used in the pasta sauces served with the traditional MACCHERONI ALLA CHITARRA. Look out for cheeses such as CACIOCAVALLO and PECORINO, made from ewes' and goats' milk, and do try the SCAMORZA from Rivisondoli. Grilled over a wood fire, it makes a delicious change from meat. Over on the Adriatic coast, in

Pescara, you can try *brodetto alla pescarese*, full of chilli of course, and in Vasto they make *scapece*, marinated fish coloured with saffron from L'Aquila.

The Abruzzo is also known for *digestivi* or herb-based liqueurs, of which *Centerbe* is the most famous; most restaurants will put several bottles on the table at the end of the meal. CONFETTI (coloured sugared almonds) are a speciality of Sulmona, and cakes made from almonds and walnuts can be found all over, every town having its own speciality.

Campania

Tomatoes, grown all over the south of Italy, were first canned and made into purée in Campania.

The most common pasta dish is *spaghetti al pomodoro* (with tomato) or *pummarola*, in Neapolitan dialect, but another firm favourite is *spaghetti con aglio e olio* (with garlic and oil). More elaborate sauces, such as RAGÙ NAPOLETANO or beef with onions called LA GENOVESE (which, despite its name –'the Genoese'– is Neapolitan) are usually made for Sunday lunch. Inland, you can find the traditional MINESTRA MARITATA, a type of soup, and the highly spiced offal dish, SOFFRITTO, which is served with spaghetti or toasted bread.

Neapolitans are fond of MINESTRE, thick soups made from pasta and pulses such as beans, chick-peas and lentils. Also popular are pasta with vegetables, like PASTA E PATATE, PASTA E PISELLI and PASTA E CAVOLFIORE, which are so filling they make a one-course meal. An alternative to pasta is SARTÙ DI RISO, a really rich rice pie originating from the reign of the Bourbons. Made on special occasions, it is difficult to find outside the home.

Fish obviously plays a large part in Neapolitan cuisine, especially the octopus and squid caught in the Bay of Naples. ZUPPA DI COZZE, *spaghetti alle vongole veraci* (*vongole veraci* are true clams, a particular, large variety that have small 'horns' protruding from their shells) and POLPI AFFOGATI (octopus in a spicy tomato sauce) are three most popular dishes, not to mention the delicious roast fish.

The local cheeses, such as PROVOLONE, SCAMORZA and CACIOCAVALLO, are worth tasting, but the real delicacy is the MOZZARELLA DI BUFALA. Around Salerno you can still find *burielli*, mini mozzarella cheeses covered with cream and sold in earthenware jars. (Unfortunately, they would not survive a journey!) Should you be staying in a Neapolitan household, you may be treated to a *pizza rustica*, a pizza-pie filled with anything from greens cooked with garlic, to eggs and salami. The bars and cake shops sell RUSTICI, with a sweet pastry case and a savoury filling, and TARALLI (savoury, ring-shaped biscuits). The real sweet treats are the SFOGLIATELLE (sweet ricotta-filled cakes) in two versions, either *ricce* or *frolle* (made with puff or shortcrust pastry). Should you ever be in Naples at Easter time, you can also try the PASTIERA or, at Christmas, the STRUFFOLI.

Apulia

Apulia (Puglia) was once almost entirely covered with sheep. Now the plain has been claimed for agriculture, mainly cultivation of durum wheat and vegetables. These are then made into pasta and its accompanying vegetable sauces, such as ORECCHIETTE CON CIME DI RAPA (turnip tops), one of the most famous local dishes. Vegetables are also used in the TIELLA (local dialect for *teglia* or baking tin). You can find *tielle* in which ingredients such as sardines or lamb are layered with potatoes and vegetables and baked in the oven. The *tiella di riso e cozze* has the unusual combination of mussels, potatoes and rice.

Apulia, being almost a peninsula, is famous for its fish. The shellfish farms in the Gulf of Taranto produce not only excellent mussels but also the sought-after oyster. The tiny TRIGLIE (red mullet), which live among the rocks along the coast, are really special when barbecued, while the fresh anchovies, when fried and seasoned, can easily compete with the more sophisticated roast sea bass. Bari, on the Adriatic coast, is famous for its *polpi arricciati* ('curled' octopus) which are subjected to a beating and whirling in special baskets to make them curl.

You cannot leave Apulia without tasting its golden olive oil which is often thought of as being rather rich by northerners. It is, of course, used generously in all local dishes and in the making of bread and the bread-like pizza FOCACCIA.

The local production of almonds influences the type of cakes and pastries made.

Apulia is heaven for fish-lovers

THE REGIONS OF ITALY

Basilicata and Calabria

These two mountainous regions, stretching down into the toe of Italy, are known as the 'deep south'. Tourism, unfortunately, has encouraged hotels and restaurants, especially those on the coast, to serve 'national' dishes. You have to go inland to sample traditional regional cuisine. Home-made pasta types, made to old recipes, include *strascinati* (rolled over specially carved boards) and *fusilli* (wrapped around knitting needles to make spirals). They are served with rich RAGÙ sauces, made from chopped lamb, veal and tomatoes and, of course, PEPERONCINO which is added to everything in handfuls! This habit of highly seasoning everything with chillies dates back to the time when they were eaten whole to ward off illnesses. *Sugna piccante*, made from pork dripping, salt, fennel seeds

A Calabrian olive grove

and lots of chilli, is used for flavouring sauces or soups, or may be just spread on bread. Pork is the main meat, and every bit of the pig is used; even the blood is not wasted, going to make SANGUINACCIO (a dense chocolate spread!). SALSICCE (sausages), spiced with black pepper and chilli, are found everywhere and eaten raw, fried, grilled, roasted, dried, smoked or pickled in olive oil to keep them moist. According to Cicero, the sausage was invented in Basilicata (or Lucania as it is also known); in fact, sausage is often called *luganica*, from 'Lucania'. The CAPOCOLLO, PEZZENTA and SOPPRESSATA, all locally cured meats, are excellent.
The other common meat is lamb; and dairy products are made mainly from ewes' milk. RICOTTA, with a salted version

called *ricotta forte*, CACIOCAVALLO and PECORINO are the more common cheeses, along with the buttery BURRINI.

Down on the coast the fish soup is full of chilli, and an unusual type of 'caviar', called *mestica*, is made from newly hatched anchovies mixed with chilli and oil.

Calabria has its own type of pizza called PITTA, which is stuffed or topped with almost anything, including fish and highly seasoned pork offal. The high plains of the Calabrian Sila range provide delicious mushrooms almost all year round, while the low plains around Santa Eufemia, Sibari and Rosarno produce fruit and vegetables of which the shiny, purple aubergine is the queen.

Locally dried figs, almonds and honey are used to make regional cakes and pastries. *Mostaccioli*, biscuits flavoured with honey and wine, are shaped into saints, fish or animals.

Sicily

Sicily (Sicilia) offers a true Mediterranean cuisine based on olive oil, pasta, fresh fish, fruit, vegetables and herbs. The island is famed for its pasta dishes such as PASTA CON LE SARDE or *pasta alla Norma*, the latter in honour of Vincenzo Bellini, who composed the famous opera *Norma*. The most curious pasta dish, however, is *spaghetti al nero di seppie*, coloured pitch black by cuttlefish ink.

Arab influence can be found in the fish soup from Trápani called *cuscusu*, served with saffron-flavoured semolina. Trápani is probably better known, however, for its fresh tuna, baked, barbecued or fried with onions to make *tonno alla cipollata*. Messina is famous for its PESCE SPADA (swordfish) which are caught in the Straits of Messina. The local dishes are PESCE SPADA ALLA GRIGLIA and PESCE SPADA ALLA GHIOTTA, while the sardines caught all around the island are served as SARDE A 'BECCAFICU' (boned, stuffed and fried).

Meat dishes are less characteristic but the typical FARSU MAGRU (stuffed meat roll) is well worth a mention. Vegetables play a large part in Sicilian cuisine, aubergines and tomatoes taking the leading roles. Together they can be found in the sweet and sour dish CAPONATA. Sicilians love sweet foods, and their CANNOLI SICILIANI (rolled biscuits filled with ricotta cheese, candied fruit and chocolate), CASSATA SICILIANA (light sponge cake with a ricotta cheese filling) and *fruttini siciliani* (marzipan fruits and vegetables) are famous all over Italy. Lovers of savoury snacks can choose an ARANCINO (rice ball) or get some tasty *pane e meuza* (bread slices or rolls filled with charcoal-grilled pork offal – usually lights – which is highly seasoned, sometimes with chilli) from a street stall in the old town and then move on for a freshly squeezed SPREMUTA (fruit juice).

THE REGIONS OF ITALY

Popular seaside fare on Sardinia

Sardinia

In the mountainous regions of Sardinia (Sardegna) the people still live mainly as shepherds, while on the coast the tourist yachts lie anchored. Crayfish or lobster dominate the coastal menus, but traditional dishes are found inland, where even the bread is made to suit the shepherd's needs – it is thin, crisp and it breaks easily, ideal for carrying into the fields in quantity and unlikely to become stale quickly. Bread-making is one of the oldest traditions in Sardinia, where special bread is shaped into animals, flowers, or churches for weddings, into lace for christenings and is made from wholemeal flour for funerals as a sign of mourning. PORCEDDU (suckling pig) is barbecued 'shepherd style' over a wood fire. For a *festa*, larger animals were sometimes roasted whole, one inside the other like Russian dolls, in a pit dug in the ground. Unfortunately, it is difficult to find barbecued meats, apart from lamb, along the tourist track. The cured meats, however, are more accessible as they can be bought in the village stores. Hams are made from pork or wild boar, and the local sausage, highly peppered and flavoured with fennel seeds and wine vinegar, is hung next to the fireplace to be lightly smoked. It can be eaten raw, grilled or, cooked in tomato sauce, served with the small ribbed pasta shells called MALLOREDDUS. Local cheeses such as *fiore sardo* or fresh RICOTTA are naturally made from ewes' milk.

Many typical fish dishes were brought to Sardinia by invaders; for instance, the fish soup found in Cagliari called CASSOLA is of Spanish origin. BURIDDA, which in Genoa is a soup, here becomes fish poached in vinegar solution and topped with nuts. In Cala Gonone, you can taste *spaghetti al sugo di granchio* (spaghetti with crab sauce). A typical Sardinian speciality is BOTTARGA (salted and dried fish roes), offered as a starter or crumbled over spaghetti. Sardinian sweets are easily found. SEADAS (a kind of cheese tart) or individually wrapped almond *sospiri* are often served in tourist restaurants, whereas *pabassinas*, iced sultana cakes decorated with coloured sugar strands, can be bought in supermarkets.

A–Z GUIDE TO ITALIAN FOOD

A

◆◆◆Abbacchio

Roman spring lamb. In other parts of Italy it is called AGNELLO. Slaughtered between three and 12 months old, they are very tender, being still unweaned. A whole animal may weigh as little as 5kg/10lb. In Rome, there are special butchers' shops selling only lamb, chicken and eggs, called *abbacchi e polli*; here lamb carcases are hung from the ceiling waiting to be sold whole, cut in half or by the kilo.

◆◆◆Abbacchio alla cacciatora

Hunter-style lamb, a Roman dish. It is chopped into small pieces and cooked until golden with olive oil, garlic and rosemary, then sprinkled with wine vinegar.

◆◆◆Abbacchio alla scottadito

Tender chops, grilled over a wood or charcoal fire. They are meant to be picked up and eaten with your fingers – carefully, or you will do as their name suggests and 'burn your finger'!

◆◆Abbacchio arrosto

Lamb roasted in the oven with rosemary and garlic. It is a typical Roman dish, a favourite for Sunday lunch, especially at Easter time. Legs or shoulders of lamb are roasted whole, cut into portions and served on the bone. The meat is so tender that it melts in your mouth.

Acciughe

Anchovy fillets. They are used to flavour and garnish pizzas and to enrich many fish-based sauces. Also delicious served with butter and crackers or bread as a starter. Anchovies can be bought ready prepared in small bottles or cans, but the best ones are those still under salt at the grocer's. Rinse them in a little vinegar to remove the salt, then serve them in olive oil with chopped garlic and oregano.

Aceto di vino

Wine vinegar. There are many different types of wine vinegar available, some of which are flavoured with herbs. Most households make their own wine vinegar by keeping a special bottle where they pour the dregs of all their wine. The presence of a small piece of pasta ensures that the wine turns into vinegar. It is difficult to find malt vinegar.

◆◆◆Acqua cotta

Thin vegetable soup made from onions, garlic, celery, carrots, peppers and tomatoes, served in terracotta bowls lined wih croûtons. It is sometimes served with an egg poached in it. This dish from the Tuscan Maremma is really warming on cold days.

Aglio

Garlic. It is used extensively in Italian cooking, and garlic-sellers can always be found in the markets with their strings of the pungent bulb to hang in the kitchen. Garlic does not last forever, however, and tends to turn into mould if not kept in a cool dry place.

Agnello

Lamb.

♦♦Agnello al forno or **tiella di agnello**

Spring lamb, cut into chunks and baked in the oven with potatoes, onions, tomatoes, garlic, olive oil and white wine and seasoned with ground black pepper and oregano. This way of roasting lamb is typical of Naples and the south.

♦Agnolotti

Squares of freshly made pasta. Similar to ravioli, they are usually stuffed with ricotta cheese and spinach. They are sometimes stuffed with meat, especially in the north, and are then usually served in a tomato and basil sauce.

Agrodolce

Sweet and sour. Vegetables such as red peppers, onions and courgettes are sometimes served in this way, cooked in a vinegar solution with the addition of sugar. They are then glazed with the sauce before serving.

Albicocche

Apricots. They are in season for most of the summer. The larger ones, despite their deliciously tempting appearance, are sometimes quite tasteless and it is often better to select the smaller fruit. Ask if you can choose your own; you often can, especially in the south.

Alici

Fresh anchovies.

♦♦♦Alici dorate e fritte

Fresh anchovies, dipped in seasoned flour and beaten egg, then fried in olive oil until golden. They are served with wedges of lemon and a crisp green salad. A delicious but cheap fish dish.

Amarene

Sour cherries. Used to make jams and the deliciously thick syrup or conserve which is sometimes poured over vanilla ice-cream.

♦Amaretti

Bitter almond macaroons. Sometimes served with drinks or used for making cakes and desserts. They are also one of the unusual ingredients in the FRITTO MISTO served in Piedmont.

♦♦♦Amatriciana, all'

Sauce made with tomatoes, bacon, onion and chillies. Traditionally served with BUCATINI (spaghetti-like pasta) and sprinkled with grated pecorino cheese (see recipe on page 100).

♦♦Anatra in porchetta

Duck stuffed with finely chopped duck's liver, bacon or ham, rosemary, garlic and fennel. It is roasted in the oven, basted with white wine, until tender. Often found in Tuscany and Umbria.

Anguilla

Freshwater eel. Found in most rivers and lakes, *anguille* are cooked in many different ways depending on local tradition. They can either be seasoned with various herbs and spices and cooked in chunks on the spit, or casseroled with or without tomatoes. *Anguille* are bred in abundance in the Comácchio Valley where they are one of the traditional regional dishes.

♦♦♦Anguilla alla comácchio

Skinned eel cooked in a pan

with chopped onion, rosemary and a sprinkling of vinegar. Tomatoes and seasoning are then added. When the eel is cooked and the sauce thick, it is served with POLENTA.

◆◆◆Anguria
Watermelon. These vary in size and shape from the smaller, dark green, round ones, weighing approximately 2kg/4lb, to the larger, oblong, yellow and green striped ones, weighing up to 10kg/20lb each. From June through to September, enormous piles of watermelons appear at the roadsides up and down the country. They are guarded 24 hours a day by watermelon vendors, sleeping in rough shacks built among the fruit. Watermelons are also sold by the slice on street stalls in the cities, cooled with blocks of ice. 'Mangi, bevi e ti lavi la faccia!' 'You eat, drink and wash your face!' – a good Italian description of consuming this refreshing fruit!

Antipasto
Hors d'oeuvres. There are many different types of antipasto, or starters, ranging from the antipasto all'italiana or antipasto misto – a selection of sliced meats and cheeses, served with olives, pickles and anchovy fillets (see recipe on page 98) – to the more sophisticated fish and seafood salads. Some of the more common are: BRUSCHETTA, INSALATA DI MARE, OLIVE ASCOLANE, piatto freddo (similar to antipasto all'italiana), PROSCIUTTO E MELONE and tartine al tartufo (canapés with truffles).

◆Aragosta
Crayfish. Although the dictionary translation is crayfish, many people mistakenly call it lobster. Sardinia is the main Italian producer but, even there, aragosta is still expensive. When fresh, crayfish are delicious poached and served very simply with olive oil and lemon or mayonnaise. Most fish restaurants keep their crayfish alive in tanks of seawater and customers are invited to choose their own.

Arance
Oranges. An orange tree, laden with bright orange fruit hanging among the dark green leaves, is a wonderful sight when spotted for the first time. Another memorable experience is the penetrating perfume of the orange groves in blossom in spring, at sunset. Italy produces oranges of all types, from the juicy tarocchi

Home-grown Italian oranges

A–Z GUIDE TO ITALIAN FOOD

Relaxing in a Roman restaurant

with thin, shiny peel, and the *sanguinelle* (blood oranges) to the extra sweet *vaniglia* (vanilla oranges) which come from Sicily. The first oranges start to arrive in the markets in November and last right through the winter and spring.

♦♦♦Arancini
Savoury rice balls. They are not always round being sometimes shaped like a pointed orange. They are made from boiled rice mixed with butter and grated Parmesan cheese, left to cool and then moulded into shape. A spoonful of rich meat sauce and peas is put in the middle of each ball, which is then coated in egg and breadcrumbs and fried. Found in most bars and *rosticcerie* in Sicily, where they are a delicious traditional snack.

♦Arista di maiale
Boned loin of pork, seasoned with garlic, rosemary and fennel. The name of the dish comes from the Greek *arista*,

meaning 'the best'. The meat is either roasted in the oven or on the spit. Most restaurants serve slices of it with potatoes roasted in the same tin. This delicious Tuscan main course can also be found in other parts of central and northern Italy.

♦♦♦Arrabbiata, all'
Sauce made with tomatoes, oil, garlic and lots of chillies. Traditionally served with PENNE (pasta quills) and sprinkled with chopped parsley. Very spicy, it is recommended for curry lovers (see recipe on page 102).

♦Arrosto misto
Mixed roast meats. Compared to some of the other exciting items on the menu, this dish may look rather boring. However, when it includes crispy golden piglet, tender spring lamb, roast veal and one or two local sausages it competes very well. This is especially the case when all

the meats, fragrantly seasoned with herbs, have been barbecued over glowing embers and kept moist by basting with wine throughout the cooking.

◆Arrosto morto
Pot roast. A lean piece of young beef or veal is cooked with oil, butter and wine on a bed of chopped onions, carrots, celery and mushrooms. These vegetables form the sauce served with pasta as a first course. This dish is usually made at home.

◆Asiago
A cheese produced in the north of Italy on the high plain of Asiago. It has a spongy appearance (it is full of tiny holes) and a mild flavour and is made in large round cheeses which are cut to order.

Asparagi
Asparagus. Despite Italy's being one of the main producers of asparagus, the price never seems to fall very low. At its best in April and May, it is sold in the shops and markets tied in bundles. Asparagus is usually served boiled and dressed with olive oil and lemon juice or topped with a fried egg. It is also used in risottos, pasta sauces and omelettes.

◆Asparagi alla parmigiana
Asparagus coated with melted butter and grated Parmesan cheese. This rich dish is from Emilia–Romagna.

Astice
Lobster. This is the real lobster with its two large nippers, as opposed to crayfish. See ARAGOSTA for serving suggestions.

B

◆◆◆Bacalà alla vicentina
Dried cod (STOCCAFISSO) simmered with onions and milk for several hours until the sauce becomes thick and creamy. It is then served with slices of fried POLENTA.

◆◆Bacalà mantecato
Dried cod (STOCCAFISSO), whisked with garlic and olive oil to form a thick creamy paste. Served cold with toast or POLENTA. This unusual strong-flavoured dish from Veneto, is not to everyone's taste.

◆◆◆Baccalà
Salted cod. These strong-smelling fillets are found all over Italy. On Fridays, a traditional 'fish' day, you can buy them already soaked, ready to be transformed into one of the many regional dishes that include them. Coated in batter and deep fried as crunchy *filetti di baccalà*, they are served in Roman pizzerias. In Veneto, dried cod – STOCCAFISSO is called *bacalà* (with one 'c') which can cause confusion. However, the two kinds of cured fish (salted and dried) are very similar.

◆◆◆Bagna caöda
An oily dip strongly flavoured with garlic and anchovies. It is served in a special pot, over a burner, placed in the centre of the table, with a selection of raw and cooked vegetables. In Piedmont these 'dipped' vegetables, served with crusty bread, make a good starter or light lunch.

Bagnet
Sauces in Piedmont, served with boiled meats, fish or eggs.

◆Bagnet di pomodori
A sieved tomato sauce spiced with chillies and vinegar.

◆Bagnet verde
Sauce made from chopped parsley, anchovy fillets and garlic, mixed with breadcrumbs, vinegar and olive oil.

Basilico
Basil. Fresh basil is used extensively in Italian cooking and is readily obtainable from greengrocers from spring through to late autumn. The ideal herb for dressing tomatoes and the basis of PESTO GENOVESE.

◆Bel Paese
A cheese with a mild taste and creamy texture. The round, flat cheeses from Lombardy are wrapped in foil depicting a map of Italy, the *bel paese* (beautiful country).

◆Bigné
Cream puffs filled with custard cream or ZABAIONE. They are found in all cake shops, in various flavours and sizes.

◆◆◆Bigné di San Giuseppe
Similar to BIGNÉ, but fried, filled with custard cream and dredged with icing sugar. Traditionally, they are eaten to celebrate St Joseph's day on 19 March, but they start appearing in the shops soon after New Year.

Bigoli
A special type of spaghetti, using hard-wheat, wholemeal flour, made from an old recipe handed down from the housewives of Bassano del Grappa.

Bistecca
Beef steaks from various cuts, such as sirloin, T-bone and rump.

◆◆Bistecca alla fiorentina
T-bone steak from Tuscany. To be *alla fiorentina*, the meat should come from the Chianina herd (known for their size and the quality meat they yield), be about 2.5cm/1 inch thick, weigh between 500–800g/1–1¾lb and be grilled over a wood or charcoal fire.

◆Bistecca alla pizzaiola
A rump or sirloin steak cooked in tomato and oregano sauce similar to that used for pizzas, hence its description, *alla pizzaiola* – 'in the style of the pizza-maker'. Originates from Naples (see recipe on page 102).

◆◆Bitto
A cheese from the Valtellina valley in Lombardy, made from a mixture of cows' and goats' milk. It has a firm texture and slightly 'musty' flavour. Look out for it in the local shops and markets.

◆Bocconcini di vitello
Small, bite-sized pieces of veal cooked in wine and butter or oil. Often served with peas or mushrooms.

◆Bollito misto
A plate of mixed boiled meats from Trentino and Piedmont. These meats include chicken, knuckle of veal, beef, ox tongue and sausage, all sliced and served with boiled potatoes and onions. *Salsa verde* (green sauce), made from chopped parsley, basil, garlic and capers, is the traditional accompaniment to

this interesting option for the out-of-season traveller.

◆◆◆Bolognese, alla
Sauce made with tomatoes, minced beef, carrot, celery and onion. Traditionally served with fresh pasta and grated Parmesan.

◆◆Bonet
Delicious chocolate-flavoured, milk puddings. They contain crushed bitter almond macaroons and are coated with a caramel sauce. A real treat for sweet-toothed visitors to Piedmont.

Borlotti
A type of bean which can be dried, canned or found fresh in the summer. They are mottled red and white, turn brown on cooking, and are used for pasta soups or served as a vegetable.

◆◆Boscaiola, alla
Woodcutter's sauce. This varies from region to region but usually contains mushrooms and ham.

◆◆◆Bottarga
Salted, dried and pressed tuna fish or mullet roes from Sardinia. Sliced very thinly and served as a starter, or crumbled over spaghetti, it has a very strong 'fishy' flavour.

◆Braciola di maiale
Loin pork chop, either fried with garlic and fennel seeds or grilled over a wood or charcoal fire.

◆◆◆Brasato al Barolo
A lean joint of beef marinated overnight (an old recipe recommends eight days!) in red BAROLO wine, herbs and spices, then braised slowly until tender. The meat and its deliciously rich sauce is served in Piedmont with potato purée or POLENTA (see recipe on page 105).

◆◆◆Bresaola
Dried fillet of beef from the Valtellina valley in the Italian Alps. It is served sliced thinly, dressed with olive oil, lemon juice, ground black pepper and parsley. Served with crusty bread, it makes a delicious starter or even a main course in the summer.

◆◆Broccoletti
A dark green, leafy vegetable similar to turnip tops. It can sometimes be rather bitter, but is delicious served cold with olive oil and lemon juice or sautéed with garlic and chillies.

◆◆◆Brodetto di pesce
Fish soup. It varies, in content and name, from region to region. In Veneto it is called brodeto, while in the south it is ZUPPA DI PESCE, which usually includes shellfish.

◆◆◆Brodetto di pesce alla marchigiana
Fish soup from the Marches.

Borlotti beans

It is made from up to 16 different types of fish, cooked with stock, tomatoes, fennel and a dash of vinegar and served with croûtons.

◆Brodo
A thin meat broth or consommé. Served as a soup with small pasta shapes (*pastina*) or stuffed pasta (TORTELLINI), or used to make risottos.

◆◆Bross
A sort of 'potted' cheese from Piedmont. A mixture of local cheeses is creamed together with GRAPPA and wine to spread on bread.

◆◆◆Bruschetta
Garlic toast. This is a typical Roman starter. Delicious eaten piping hot with sliced, cured ham and accompanied by a glass of cool wine from the Castelli Romani (see recipe on page 97).

◆◆Brutti e buoni
Small almond rock cakes found in Umbria and Tuscany. They are called 'ugly and good' because, despite their ugly appearance, they are delicious!

Bucatini
Type of pasta, similar to spaghetti but with a hole running through the centre. Known as *perciatelli* in the south.

◆Budino
This milk pudding is similar to blancmange and is usually flavoured with chocolate or vanilla. A favourite with children.

◆◆◆Buridda
A fish dish. In Liguria, it is a stew, dating back to the Saracens, made from mixed fish cooked in tomato sauce with vegetables, anchovy fillets and pine kernels. In Sardinia, however, it is a dish of tuna or rock salmon steaks topped with a mixture of breadcrumbs, chopped nuts, garlic and nutmeg. A must for the fish lover.

◆◆Burrini or butirri
Small CACIOCAVALLO cheeses from the south with butter in their centre.

◆Burro, al
Freshly cooked pasta mixed with butter and a little pasta water and served with grated Parmesan. Hardly ever appears on menus, but can always be asked for in restaurants. Simple but delicious when made well.

◆◆◆Busecca
A Milanese dish made from tripe. The tripe is cut into thin strips, sautéed in butter with vegetables and sage, and cooked in tomato sauce until tender; then cooked large white butter beans are added. Served generously sprinkled with grated Parmesan and black pepper.

C

Cacciatora, alla
'Hunter style'. Meat, such as lamb, chicken or rabbit, cooked with olive oil, garlic and rosemary, and sprinkled with wine vinegar.

◆◆◆Cacciucco
A rich fish soup from Leghorn (Livorno) in Tuscany. Fish, molluscs and shellfish are casseroled with tomatoes,

garlic, chillies and red wine. It is served on a bed of croûtons in individual terracotta bowls. Delicious!

◆Cachi
Persimmons. Pronounced *kaakee*, these are an unusual, very sweet fruit with a rather 'slimy' texture. They are in season in late summer.

◆◆Cacio e pepe
A simple sauce made with grated pecorino cheese and lashings of freshly ground black pepper.

◆◆Cacio e uova
With cheese and egg. Beaten egg and grated cheese are added to vegetables such as courgettes (*zucchini cacio e uova*) or to lamb (*agnello cacio e uova*), while hot, to make a thick coating sauce.

◆Caciocavallo
Pear-shaped cows' milk cheeses from the south. Their name comes from the practice of stringing them together in pairs and hanging them *a cavallo* (astride) over wooden beams to mature. Their flavour varies from mild to strong, depending on maturity. See also BURRINI.

◆Caciotta
Cheeses made from ewes' milk. They have a mild flavour and a softish texture. Excellent eaten with olives.

Calamari
Squid. When preparing this popular, though strange-looking mollusc, be careful to remove the head, eyes, transparent cartilage and ink sack (full of very black ink) before cooking. Sold whole or sliced into rings, it is cooked in tomato sauce, grilled or fried.

Caciocavallo *cheeses, riding high*

◆◆◆Calamari fritti
Deep fried squid. Rings and tentacles of squid are dipped in a light batter and deep fried. Though rather 'rubbery' to the bite they have an interesting fishy taste. Often served mixed with fried prawns.

◆◆Calamari ripieni
Stuffed squid. The squid is stuffed with a mixture of breadcrumbs, parsley, garlic, anchovies and capers, then cooked in olive oil and white wine.

◆◆◆Calzoni
A type of pizza. It is folded in half and filled with cooked ham or salami, mozzarella and

ricotta cheese, then baked in the oven. Served as an alternative to pizza.

♦♦♦Canederli
Small, light dumplings. Made from breadcrumbs flavoured with smoked ham and sausage, they are cooked and served in consommé in Trentino–Alto Adige. Really warming on a cool evening.

Cannellini
Small, white haricot beans which are dried, canned or found fresh in the summer. They are both used as a vegetable and made into delicious soups with pasta.

♦Cannelloni
Freshly-made rolls of pasta stuffed with various fillings, coated with sauce and baked in the oven. The commonest version has a minced beef filling, is coated with *bolognese* sauce, topped with white sauce and sprinkled with grated Parmesan. Can easily make a filling one-course meal when followed by a salad.

Capitone, *a southern delicacy*

♦♦♦Cannoli siciliani
Crisp fried rolls that look like brandy snaps. A Sicilian delight, they are filled with sweetened ricotta cheese, candied peel and pieces of chocolate. Except in the really hot months of July and August, they can be bought from most good cake shops.

♦Cantucci
Nut-filled biscuits, served with a glass of Vin Santo (sweet wine) after a meal in Tuscany.

Capellini
Very fine spaghetti. It is usually served to children in tomato sauce or broken into consommé.

♦Capitone
Sea-water eel. Found in the south, it is traditionally cooked in tomato sauce and eaten in Naples at Christmas.

♦♦Capocollo
A Calabrian salami. It is made with cuts of pork from the neck and shoulder, smoked inside a pig's bladder and pickled in olive oil. Delicious, especially when home-made.

♦♦♦Caponata
A Sicilian sweet and sour dish. In its simplest form, it is made from aubergines and tomatoes mixed with capers, pine kernels, sultanas and olives, and flavoured with vinegar and sugar. It can be 'dressed up' to include even lobster. Served both hot and cold.

Capperi
Capers. The pickled flower buds of a bush-like shrub which grows wild on rock faces exposed to the sun. Capers can be pickled in either vinegar or salt, but in the latter case they must be

rinsed well before using. Used to flavour many Italian sauces.

◆◆Cappon magro
Ornate fish and vegetable dish. This bed of diced vegetables, piled high with poached fish coated in green sauce, garnished with hard-boiled eggs, pickles, artichokes and peeled shrimps and topped with a whole crayfish and a dozen or so oysters, has to be seen to be believed! A traditional *maigre* (for days of fasting) dish from Liguria.

Capretto
Baby goat.

◆◆Capretto arrosto
Roast baby goat. In this typical dish from the south, the goat is cut into small pieces and baked (although *arrosto* means roasted) in the oven with potatoes, onions, tomatoes, peas and wine. Eaten at Easter.

◆◆◆Carbonade
Salted beef dish from Valle d'Aosta. The beef is cooked in wine and onions, seasoned with grated nutmeg and served with POLENTA. Called *carbonade* because it is as black as coal. Unfortunately it is often made from fresh beef nowadays.

◆◆◆Carbonara, alla
Piping hot spaghetti mixed with beaten eggs, grated Parmesan and pecorino cheeses, freshly ground black pepper and crunchy, fried chopped bacon. A 'must' for bacon and egg lovers who find themselves in Rome.

Carciofi
Artichokes. These are a very common spring vegetable.

They are eaten from February or March through to May when they are young. The hairy choke will not have developed inside the bud, so preparation is simple compared to the method used for mature artichokes. The outside leaves are pulled off and discarded, then the remaining leaves and stalk are trimmed; the rest is ready for cooking and eating. Choose those that are firm and not too open and 'spiky'.

◆◆◆Carciofi alla Giudia
Jewish-style artichokes. A speciality of the restaurants in the old Jewish ghetto in Rome, they are opened out like a flower, plunged into boiling oil, then served crisp and piping hot. They literally melt in your mouth.

◆◆◆Carciofi alla romana
Roman-style artichokes. They are stuffed with garlic, parsley and mint, then braised until tender. Often chosen as a main course by vegetarians.

◆◆Carciofi dorati e fritti
Wedges of artichokes, dipped in flour and beaten egg, then fried in olive oil.

◆Carpaccio
Paper-thin slices of raw beef dressed with lemon juice and olive oil and served with slivers of Parmesan cheese and RUGHETTA. Do not be put off because the meat is raw – it is really delicious.

Cartoccio
Food baked in foil or a sealed bag.

◆◆◆Cassata siciliana
A Sicilian dessert made from sweetened ricotta cheese, candied peel and chocolate chips on a sponge base,

covered with green almond paste and icing. The dessert is decorated with whole glacé fruits. Extremely sweet but delicious.

◆◆◆Cassoeula

An ancient Milanese dish made from spare ribs of pork and cabbage casseroled with vegetables. Served with POLENTA. It is traditionally eaten in winter, especially on 17 January, to celebrate St Anthony's Day (he apparently kept pigs!).

◆◆◆Cassola

An unusual fish soup, found in Cagliari on Sardinia. Made from fish and octopus casseroled with dried tomatoes, onions, garlic and chillies, it is served on croûtons in individual dishes.

◆Castagnaccio

A traditional Tuscan cake made from chestnut flour, pine kernels and sultanas. It is baked in large flat tins and cut into slices.

Castagne

Chestnuts. In the autumn, hot-chestnut sellers sit on street corners with glowing braziers and sell bags of roasted chestnuts. Chestnuts are also used for making cakes and are sometimes served as a vegetable.

◆Castagnole

Tiny balls of fried dough coated in castor sugar and sometimes filled with custard cream. One of the many sweets served at *carnevale* time (before Lent).

◆Castrato

Mutton. Served as grilled chops or as the stew, with vegetables and tomatoes,

which makes the thick sauce served to accompany pasta in the Marches, Abruzzo and Latium.

◆Ceci

Chick-peas, either dried or canned. They are flavoured with rosemary and served as a vegetable in some parts of central Italy, and with pasta in Rome. Friday is the traditional day for *pasta e ceci* in the Roman *osterie*.

◆Cervella

Calves' brains. They are either sautéed in butter or cut into bite-sized pieces and coated in batter, then fried. Can be found in FRITTO MISTO or sometimes served with fried artichokes.

◆Charlotte

Dessert made from very light sponge cakes sandwiched together with freshly whipped cream. One of the most common sweets served in restaurants.

◆◆Chiacchiere

Strips of fried dough-like pastry, coated in honey and icing sugar. Traditionally served at *carnevale* time (before Lent).

◆◆Chiodini

Small mushrooms with a long stalk and tiny head – hence their name, 'little nails'. They grow in mountain valleys, and are delicious served as a vegetable, with pasta or pickled in oil and vinegar.

◆◆◆Cialzons alla Carnia

Sweet and sour AGNOLOTTI (pasta squares) from Friuli, served as a first course. Stuffed with spinach mixed with chocolate, sultanas and candied peel!

◆◆◆Cialzons friulani
Sweet and sour AGNOLOTTI (pasta squares) from Friuli, stuffed with mashed potatoes flavoured with cinammon, sugar, parsley and mint. Served with melted butter and grated cheese.

◆Ciambelle or ciambelline
Ring-shaped home-made biscuits, usually made with wine. They are often served in *trattorie* at the end of a meal and are excellent dipped in wine. 'Dunking' is not frowned upon in Italy!

◆◆Cicoria
A dark green, leafy vegetable with a rather bitter taste. It can be found growing wild in fields. Served sautéed in oil and garlic or cooked in tomato sauce, it is a Roman speciality.

◆Cima ripiena
A 'pocket' of veal stuffed with beaten egg, cheese and vegetables from Liguria. Served sliced, hot or cold.

Temptation for a sweet tooth

◆◆◆Cinghiale
Wild boar. They abound in the Tuscan Maremma where they are served barbecued, stewed in tomato sauce and served with pasta, or made into hams, salami or sausages. The meat has a stronger flavour than pork, but should be tried.

Cioccolatini
Chocolates. Italy has an excellent reputation for its chocolates, which are exported all over the world. Some of the more interesting ones to try are *Baci* or 'kisses', with chopped hazelnuts; *Gianduiotti*, creamy hazelnut-flavoured truffled chocolates; *Kinder*, milk chocolate fingers with a creamy white filling which children love; and *Pocket Coffee* filled with liquid coffee.

◆◆Ciociara, alla
Sauce made with cream,

mushrooms, chopped cooked ham and peas. Traditionally served with ribbon-shaped pasta.

◆◆◆Ciuppin
A sieved fish soup from Liguria, similar to the French *bouillabaisse*.

Cocco
Coconut. It heralds the arrival of summer with its appearance on street stalls, where it is sold in slices stacked under a 'fountain' of running water to keep it fresh.

Cocomero
The Roman name for ANGURIA (watermelon).

◆◆◆Coda alla vaccinara
Oxtail stew. A real Roman dish found in the *osterie* around Testaccio (the area near the old slaughterhouse) which specialise in offal dishes.

◆Colomba
Dove-shaped cake, flavoured with candied peel and covered in flaked almonds and sugar. It is a traditional Easter treat.

Confetti
Coloured sugared almonds. They play an important part in Italian lives. These variously coloured sugared almonds are tied in small decorated bundles and given to friends and relations on special occasions. For first communions and weddings they are white, for wedding

anniversaries silver and gold, for engagements green and for graduations red.

◆◆◆Coniglio all'ischitana
A traditional rabbit dish from Ischia. On this island in the Bay of Naples there would seem to be more hunters than fishermen! The rabbit, after being marinated overnight in the local wine, is cooked with tomatoes and chillies until tender, then served with chipped potatoes.

◆◆Cornetto
A crescent-shaped sweet bread roll, or 'croissant', served for breakfast with *cappuccino*. It owes its name to its 'horn-like' shape.

Costata di manzo
Entrecôte of beef or rib steak.

◆◆◆Costoletta alla milanese
Famous egg and breadcrumbed veal cutlet from Milan. It was invented during the Italian Renaissance when it was the fashion for the rich to have their food served covered with slivers of gold. The poor dipped their cutlets in egg and breadcrumbs, then fried them in butter until golden – in colour at least! Copied by the Austrians to make *Wienerschnitzel*, this cutlet is now often served without its traditional bone (see recipe on page 105).

Italians say it with confetti

◆◆Costoletta alla valdostana
Veal cutlet with cheese stuffing. Similar to its Milanese cousin, the cutlet is, however, first stuffed with FONTINA cheese, from the Valle d'Aosta, which makes a deliciously creamy centre.

◆◆Costolette di agnello/ abbacchio
Small lamb chops, either grilled or coated in egg and breadcrumbs and deep fried.

◆◆Cotechino
A type of spicy minced pork sausage. It is boiled and served sliced with lentils.

◆◆Cotoletta alla bolognese
A thin slice of veal, coated with egg and breadcrumbs and fried, then covered with a slice of ham and cheese, topped with tomato sauce and baked in the oven. A very rich dish in true *bolognese* style.

◆◆Cozze, alle
Sauce made with mussels, with or without tomatoes. Served with spaghetti and parsley.

◆◆◆Crema di . . ., alla
A cream-based sauce. It can be made from asparagus (*crema di asparagi*), mushrooms (*crema di funghi*) walnuts (*crema di noci*), prawns (*crema di scampi*) or smoked salmon (*crema di salmone*). Usually served with fresh, ribbon-shaped pasta, such as *tagliatelle* or *tagliolini*.

◆◆◆Crema fritta
Fried custard. A Venetian dessert of shapes of thick, chilled, creamy custard, dipped in flour and fried, then dusted with sugar.

◆◆Crespelle or crêpes
Savoury pancakes filled with a mixture of ricotta and spinach, coated with tomato sauce and baked in the oven. They are an alternative to pasta. Ham, cheese and meat are also used for fillings.

◆Crocchette di patate
Fried potato croquettes. Sometimes with mozzarella cheese in the centre, they can be bought in most *pizzerie*. A tasty snack while waiting for pizza.

◆Crostata di frutta
Fresh fruit tart. The fruit is so beautifully arranged in the open pastry case that these tarts are hard to resist in the cake shop window.

◆◆Crostini
Savoury toasts. Crusty slices of bread are covered wih sliced mozzarella cheese and either Parma ham or anchovy fillets, then popped under the grill. Served in *pizzerie* as fillers.

D

Diavola, alla
Devilled. A common way of serving chicken. The chicken is halved, flattened, seasoned with herbs and ground chilli, then grilled or 'devilled' over a wood or charcoal fire.

F

Fagioli
Dried haricot or cannellini beans.

◆◆Fagioli al fiasco
Dried haricot beans cooked traditionally – slowly in a flask. Originally, Chianti wine flasks

were used; now corked glass flasks are sold specially for the purpose. The beans are served 'drowned' in olive oil as a vegetable. A Tuscan speciality.

◆◆Fagioli alla maruzzara
Cannellini beans cooked in a tomato and oregano sauce. They are mixed with pasta to make a thick soup, typical of the Campania region (see recipe on page 101).

◆◆◆Fagioli all'uccelletto
A Tuscan dish of cannellini beans cooked with garlic, sage and tomatoes, and served as a vegetable.

◆◆Fagioli con cotiche
Cannellini beans, cooked in tomato sauce and flavoured with pork rind and fat from Parma ham. A typical Roman speciality which all true Romans have tasted at least once in their lives. A cast-iron digestion is needed here, but do try them!

◆Faraona alla creta
A whole guinea fowl cooked in clay. This ancient way of cooking, used by the Longobards to keep flavour and juices in, can still be found in Lombardy.

◆◆◆Farinata
A type of pancake made in Liguria from chick-pea flour, olive oil and salt. It is baked in the oven until golden, then served piping hot generously sprinkled with freshly ground black pepper.

◆◆◆Farsu magru, falso magro
A tasty Sicilian stuffed meat roll. The filling, made from a minced beef and cheese mixture, is spread over a rectangle of veal which is then garnished with sliced hard-boiled eggs, diced cheese and crumbled sausage. It is then rolled up, tied and braised slowly with chopped onion, tomatoes and wine.

◆◆◆Fave con pecorino
Broad beans and pecorino cheese. On 1 May, the roads leading out of Rome are lined with stalls selling fresh broad beans, pecorino cheese and loaves of crusty bread, for the Romans to buy on their way to the traditional May Day picnic. This is, of course, accompanied by a bottle of wine from the Castelli.

◆◆Fegatelli di maiale
Small pieces of pig's liver, seasoned and wrapped in caul fat with bay leaves, then fried in oil and wine. A tasty dish, traditionally served with PUNTARELLE (leafy salad vegetable).

◆Fegatini di pollo
Chicken livers (or livers from other poultry). These can be sautéed in butter and served on croûtons, or made into a delicious pasta sauce called FINANZIERA.

◆◆◆Fegato alla veneziana
Thin strips of calf's liver sautéed with onions and sprinkled with white wine. A famous dish from Venice which has become a national favourite (see recipe on page 106).

Fettuccine
Thin ribbons of freshly made pasta, usually served with a RAGÙ (meat) sauce.

◆◆◆Fichi
Figs. Freshly picked figs, found in June and September, are a real treat. Peel off the

Most restaurants serve local food

green skin and enjoy the sweet jam-like fruit inside. They are also dried in the sun, sometimes stuffed with almonds or baked, to make the dried figs (*fichi secchi*) eaten at Christmas.

♦♦♦Fichi d'India
Prickly pears. They are found in the south and Sardinia in late summer. These red, orange and yellow fruits must be treated with respect as their fine thorns can be very painful! Bought from street stalls, however, already peeled, they are quite safe. In Furore, on the Amalfi coast, there is a prickly pear *festa* on the first Sunday in September.

♦♦♦Finanziera, alla
'Financier' style. A sauce made with chicken livers, onions and mushrooms cooked in white wine. In Piedmont, it includes heart, kidneys and cock's combs, too.

♦♦♦Finocchio
Fennel. This aniseed-flavoured vegetable is sliced and served in mixed salads, baked in the oven or simply served in wedges to be dipped in oil and salt to help the digestion after a rich meal. The rounder heads are referred to as 'male' (*maschi*) and they are more tender than the flatter ('female') heads.

♦♦Finocchiona
A Tuscan salami made from minced pork, seasoned with fennel seeds. Look out for it hanging in the grocers' shops or, even better, ask the butcher if he makes his own. Umbria produces a similar salami called *finocchiella*.

♦♦Fior di latte
A cheese, similar to mozzarella but made from cows' milk. A freshly made cheese, it has a rather rubbery texture and a fresh, milky flavour. It is best eaten the same day but can be kept in the refrigerator if covered with its whey or with milk.

♦♦♦Fiori di zucchini
Courgette flowers. Delicious coated in a light batter and fried. They can be stuffed with

A–Z GUIDE TO ITALIAN FOOD

mozzarella and anchovy fillets, but are good just on their own. If you decide to experiment, open them up under running water, to make sure there are no insects inside, then pat dry before coating with batter.

◆Focaccia
Very similar to pizza, but more bread-like. Usually served split in half and filled with cheese and/or salami.

◆◆◆Fonduta alla valdostana
A traditional cheese dip from Valle d'Aosta. It is made from FONTINA cheese, milk, butter and egg yolks and is served in special terracotta bowls, over burners which keep it hot, with cubes of toasted bread. Very rich and filling, but not to be · missed.

◆Fontina
A cheese made from cows' milk, produced solely in the Valle d'Aosta. The large, round, flat cheeses are salted and matured in special grottos, and only those considered perfect are stamped with the official Fontina seal. The cheese is golden yellow with a compact texture and a mild flavour which becomes stronger as it matures.

◆◆◆Fragoline
Tiny wild strawberries with a strongly scented flavour. Often sold in baskets at the roadside, they tend to be quite expensive. Only rinse them very gently before serving or they will disintegrate!

◆◆Frappe
Thin strips of fried dough-like pastry, dredged with icing sugar. Mountains of these pastries can be seen in bars and cake shops at *carnevale*

time (before Lent). They are so light that an *etto* (100g/4oz) goes a long way!

◆Freselle
Large crisp rings of biscuity bread. Used instead of croûtons or as the basis of a summer snack, *panzanella* (see recipe on page 110).

◆◆◆Friarielli
The very tips and flowers of BROCCOLETTI. In Naples, they are fried in oil and garlic and served with sausages. Very bitter tasting.

◆◆Frittata
The Italian answer to the Spanish *tortilla*. The 'filling', such as courgettes, onions or artichokes, is first chopped and cooked in the pan. Then seasoned beaten egg and grated cheese are added. It is browned on both sides and served in slices (see recipe on page 108).

◆◆Frittata con erbe
Frittata with herbs. Traditionally made from at least seven different herbs or greens picked in the fields. A dish from Friuli, it is usually made from spinach, beet tops, leeks, thyme, sage, basil and parsley. They are first boiled, then fried in oil, garlic and chopped onion before the egg is added.

◆◆◆Fritto misto all'italiana
A mixed fry. This platter of interesting-looking crisp golden morsels varies from region to region, but the basic constituents are mozzarella balls, potato croquettes, brains, tiny lamb cutlets, sliced courgettes, artichoke wedges, aubergines and cauliflower florets, all dipped in batter and deep fried.

♦♦♦Frittura di paranza

The smaller, less important fish in the catch, from the local off-shore fishing boats, fried and served with wedges of lemon. They are usually so fresh (these less prized fish do not keep), that they taste and smell of the sea!

♦♦♦Frittura di pesce

Small fish mixed with rings of squid and a few prawns, all dipped in thin batter and fried until crisp and golden. Ask for just the squid and prawns if you cannot cope with the heads and bones of the whole fish.

♦Frutti di bosco

'Woodland fruits'. This mixture of wild strawberries, raspberries, blackberries, bilberries and redcurrants is served with sugar and lemon juice or topped with freshly whipped cream and ice-cream.

♦♦♦Frutti di mare

Zoologically speaking, shellfish such as clams, mussels, scallops, razor shells and oysters. When ordering *spaghetti con frutti di mare*, however, do not be surprised if a few prawns and squid have crept in, too.

Funghi

Mushrooms. There are many different types of edible mushrooms but they all have specific names by which they are known, except the cultivated *champignons* which are called simply *funghi*.

♦♦Funghi trifolati

Sliced mushrooms sautéed in butter and garlic. They are served warm sprinkled with chopped parsley.

Wild mushrooms. Never pick your own; they are safe from the market

G

♦♦Gamberi, gamberoni

Prawns and giant prawns. They are served whole, fried with rings of squid, or grilled, or cooked with tomatoes to make a pasta sauce.

Gelato

Ice-cream (see page 44).

♦♦♦Genovese, alla

This meat and onion sauce is an old Neapolitan recipe. Served with short pasta and lots of grated Parmesan.

♦♦♦Genovese, la

A joint of beef cooked with twice its weight of onions. The onions cook down to make the delicious sauce served with pasta, while the meat is sliced and served with chipped potatoes. Despite its name, it is an ancient Neapolitan recipe.

Ghiotta, alla

A way of grilling or roasting meat or fish on the spit. It is basted with a sauce made from the fish or meat juices, mixed with olive oil, wine or vinegar, chopped ham or bacon, capers, olives, crushed anchovy fillets, garlic and cloves, all cooked in the drip tray below. This drip tray, called *leccarda*, gives its name to the dish, too.

♦♦♦Gnocchetti sardi or malloreddus
Typical Sardinian pasta in the shape of tiny GNOCCHI which look rather like shells. Served with a spicy tomato sauce.

♦♦♦Gnocchi
Unless specified otherwise, tiny cushions or rolls of very light dough made from potatoes and flour. They are cooked in boiling water and served with a tomato or meat sauce, with grated Parmesan. In the Roman *trattorie*, the set day for eating gnocchi is Thursday. Green gnocchi, mixed with spinach (*spinaci*) or nettle (*ortica*), are served with a butter or cream sauce.

The Home of Ice-cream
Iced desserts and drinks originated in the East, and Chinese cooks are said to have passed on the idea to Arabs who experimented with flavoured ice. However, credit for creating fine ices as we know them today has to be given to Italian chefs. Catherine de Medici introduced frozen delicacies to the French court in the 16th century and 100 years later the first Italian ice-cream parlour opened in Paris. An Italian chef introduced Charles I to ice-cream and the Americans were later initiated, again by the Italians.

Italy is still renowned for making some of the finest ices in the world. Even the smallest bar can offer the basic flavours of *cioccolato* (chocolate), *nocciola* (hazelnut), *vaniglia* (vanilla), *crema* (cream), *tutti frutti*, *pistacchio* (pistachio nut), *limone* (lemon), *caffè* (coffee) and *fragola* (strawberry) ice-cream. The ice-cream parlours can add at least another 20, including the bright blue *Puffi* (Smurf) type, a favourite with children. Your cone, carton or dish will often be topped with whipped cream unless you ask for it not to be – *'Senza panna, grazie'*.

◆**Gnocchi alla romana**
Roman-style gnocchi. Semolina
rounds layered with butter and
cheese, then baked in the
oven until golden.

◆**Gorgonzola**
Famous, creamy blue cheese
made from cows' milk. It is
produced in Lombardy near
the town which gave it its name
many years ago (and where it
was originally produced by
mistake!). The cheeses,
weighing 10kg/22lb each, are
left to mature and form the
characteristic dark green
mould which gives the strong
flavour. Mild Gorgonzola is
also sometimes layered with
creamy MASCARPONE.
Delicious, but very fattening!

◆◆◆**Grana**
The generic name for the hard
cheeses produced on the
Padua Plain; some are better
known as Parmesan.

◆**Granchio**
Crab. Particularly popular in
Sardinia, where crabs are
cooked in tomato sauce and
served with spaghetti. You
have to be an expert spaghetti
eater to cope with the bits of
shell which get in the way. Not
for beginners!

◆**Granoturco**
Corn on the cob. In the south it
is barbecued on the spit and
sold by the roadside.

◆**Granseola**
A large crab. Found along the
Adriatic coast from Venice to
Trieste, it is served dressed, in
its shell.

◆◆**Grigliata mista**
Mixed grill. A firm favourite in
country *trattorie* where an
open wood fire is used for
grilling meats. A standard

Grana
Hard Cheese with a
Powerful Flavour
Parmesan must be the best
known of these; however,
the fresh cheese bears no
resemblance to the dry and
dusty contents of the small
tubs lurking on the
supermarket shelves back
home. A chunk of fresh
grana has a certain
sweetness combined with
its heady flavour and
aroma. They are made
from partially skimmed
cows' milk and have a
granular texture which
gives them their name.
Depending on the
geographical region of
production, they are called
parmigiano-reggiano,
lodigiano, grana padano, or
just *grana*. The enormous
round cheeses are broken
open, never cut. It is
fascinating to watch a grocer
at work while opening a
new cheese. A special
pointed knife acts as a
lever to split the cheese in
two and then into portions.

---

mixed grill includes lamb
cutlets, pork chops, quail,
sausages and chicken, with
variations such as rabbit, spare
ribs of pork and suckling pig.

Grissini
Breadsticks. Turin is the home
of breadsticks, which were
originally made by hand all
over Piedmont. Now made
industrially, they are exported
all over the world. In Turin you
can still buy home-made ones
in some bakeries, where you

are spoilt for choice by those flavoured or enriched with spices, seeds, oil, butter and malt. Wholemeal flour may also be used.

◆Gubana
Sweet bread roll, filled with dried fruits, candied peel and nuts. This delicious bread comes from Friuli.

◆◆Gulasch
Hot, spicy meat dish, made from beef, onions and paprika. Found in the mountainous regions of Alto Adige and Friuli, it is served with boiled potatoes or POLENTA.

I

◆◆◆Impepata di cozze, 'mpepata di cozze
Mussels cooked in their own juice with the addition of chopped parsley and lashings of freshly ground black pepper. Not to be missed when on the coast around Naples or further south (see recipe on page 98).

In bianco
Plain, without sauce. On menus, pesce in bianco is poached fish, which you then dress to your liking. Italians say they are eating in bianco when not feeling too well. They dress their pasta with olive oil or butter and grated Parmesan, have their meat or fish poached or grilled, and eat their vegetables boiled.

In carpione
Usually means pickled in vinegar, wine and lemon juice after being seasoned with a mixture of herbs and spices. In Lombardy the game or fish is then served with its jelly-like sauce.

In porchetta
Roast-pork style. Game or poultry is stuffed with a mixture of chopped liver, bacon or ham, rosemary, garlic and fennel, browned in olive oil and cooked with wine until tender.

◆◆Indivia
A bitter-tasting leafy salad vegetable with thin, curly, spiky leaves, yellowish green in the centre, becoming darker towards the outside. It is also known as insalata riccia (curly salad). Displayed on the market stall, they look like curly wigs!

Insaccati
Dried sausages. Meaning 'in a sack', they include salami, and are made from spiced minced or chopped pork which is forced into different shaped 'sacks' made from natural fibres. The sausages are then salted and hung to mature in a cool, dry place.

◆◆Insalata caprese
A summer salad of mozzarella cheese, tomatoes and fresh basil. Originally from Capri, it is now a national favourite (see recipe on page 109).

◆◆◆Insalata di mare
A seafood salad, including diced octopus, squid, prawns, clams and mussels, mixed with chopped celery and garlic, then dressed with olive oil and lemon juice. Delicious when chilled and served as a starter or summer main course.

◆◆Insalata di riso
Cold rice salad. Often found in bars or tavole calde. Chilled

boiled rice is mixed with various savoury ingredients and dressed with oil and lemon or mayonnaise (see recipe on page 111).

◆Insalata mista

Mixed salad served as a side course. It usually lives up to its name and includes anything the chef decides to put in it that day.

◆Insalata verde

Green salad. An Italian green salad can be an unforgettable experience if you are lucky enough to find a country *trattoria* which serves a mixture of freshly picked leaves. You will probably have fun guessing what each one is! It is served with oil and vinegar, so if you prefer it plain tell the waiter not to dress it – *'Senza condimento, per favore'*.

◆Involtini

Stuffed meat rolls. When made from slices of beef these are similar to beef olives (rolled, stuffed, thinly sliced beef). Flavoured with garlic and parsley or carrot and celery, they are served in tomato sauce. Watch out for the cocktail stick used to secure the rolls of meat!

J

◆◆Jota

A thick soup from Friuli. Made from beans, sauerkraut and maizemeal, it is flavoured with lard, onion, sage, parsley and garlic. When meat or salami is added, it becomes a substantial one-course meal.

L

◆◆◆Lasagne

There are several regional recipes for this well-known baked pasta dish. The classic lasagne comes from Emilia–Romagna where the strips of green or white pasta are layered with BOLOGNESE sauce, white sauce and Parmesan cheese.

◆◆◆Lasagne alla napoletana

Neapolitan lasagne strips are longer and thinner and layered with RAGÙ sauce, tiny meat balls, smoked mozzarella, sliced hard-boiled eggs, salami and ricotta cheese. The ends of the strips fold over to seal the top, which is then garnished with more meat balls and diced cheese, sprinkled with Parmesan and baked until golden. Can be found on Sundays and holidays, especially around *carnevale* time (before Lent).

◆◆Latterini

Tiny poached fish dressed with oil and lemon juice. A real delicacy for fish lovers.

Lauro

Bay leaves. Used to flavour soups, stews, roast meat and liver. Fresh leaves can be picked from the bushes in parks and gardens.

◆◆Lenticchie

Lentils. Cooked either with ham, or garlic, tomatoes and parsley, they are served as a vegetable or a thick pasta soup. Lentils are traditionally eaten on New Year's Eve to bring wealth as they symbolise 'money'.

Campanian lemons are Italy's best

◆◆Lenticchie alla montanara

Lentil and chestnut soup from Abruzzo. Flavoured with bay leaves, marjoram and basil, it is served with thick slices of toasted bread.

◆◆Lepre in salmì

A very rich jugged hare. The hare is marinated and cooked in red wine with a mixture of spices. Found in Lombardy, Piedmont and Trentino, it is traditionally served with POLENTA.

Limoni

Lemons. Freshly picked lemons, with their dark green leaves, can be found on market stalls in the south. Some will have come from Amalfi, famous for its lemon groves. The very large lemons grown on Procida, one of the smaller islands in the Bay of Naples, are sliced, sprinkled with sugar and eaten as a dessert.

◆Lombata di maiale

A simple pork chop, either grilled over a wood or charcoal fire or fried in olive oil with garlic and fennel seeds.

◆◆Lonza

Like a very fatty ham or a very lean salami: it is half-way between the two. In late autumn and winter, after the pigs have been slaughtered, you can see the freshly cured *lonze*, parcelled up in brown paper and string, hanging in country butchers' shops. They have to mature in a cool dry place before being opened and sliced.

◆◆Lumache

Snails. The ancient Romans bred snails along their moss-covered city walls. They are still served in Rome, cooked in a spicy green sauce, on the eve of St John's day, 24 June. Legend has it that on this day, witches and devils surround St John's Basilica where the skull of the saint is kept. To protect themselves, the Romans used to ring the church bells, hang strings of garlic behind their doors, and eat snails, which symbolise the devil. The more snails they managed to eat the better!

M

◆◆Maccheroni alla chitarra
Freshly made pasta from Abruzzo which looks like 'square' spaghetti. It was originally made by pressing the rolled pasta dough through the strings of a *chitarra* (a series of wires stretched over a wooden frame, similar to a guitar). It is traditionally served with a chilli sauce or a rich RAGÙ, made from lamb, tomatoes, peppers and chillies.

◆Macedonia di frutta
Fresh fruit salad. This varies with the season, but can always be found on menus, dressed with sugar and lemon juice, or sometimes a sweet liqueur.

Malloreddus
See GNOCCHETTI SARDI.

Mandorle
Almonds. In the southern regions of Apulia, Calabria and Sicily, the pink and white almond blossom appears soon after Christmas. Almonds are used extensively in the production of sweets, cakes and liqueurs, not to mention the almond nougat made in Cremona which is exported all over the world.

◆Maritozzi con la panna
Sweet bread buns split in half and filled to overflowing with freshly whipped cream. Can be found in most Roman bars.

◆◆◆Marrons glacés
Large, succulent, candied chestnuts. Unfortunately, they are only available during the winter, sold loose in cake shops and boxed for giving away at Christmas.

◆Mascarpone
A cream cheese. Although classed as cheese, it tastes more like clotted cream. Delicious spread on bread or served with strawberries, it is sold loose in the grocer's and pre-packed in supermarkets. Not usually produced in July and August.

◆◆◆Mazzancolle
Giant prawns, also called GAMBERONI. They are grilled on skewers over a wood or charcoal fire. Six or eight are a normal portion, so don't order them as your main course if you are really hungry!

Melanzane
Aubergines. These are a summer vegetable which can now be found all year round; the most common are the shiny, oblong, dark purple ones. Choose those which are firm to the touch and not too large, to avoid finding them full of seeds.

◆◆Melanzane al funghetto
Diced aubergines, fried in olive oil and garlic with a little tomato and fresh basil. It is served as a vegetable in the south.

◆◆◆Melanzane alla parmigiana
A favourite summer dish made from fried aubergines layered with tomato sauce, mozzarella and grated Parmesan, then baked in the oven (see recipe on page 107).

◆◆Mesciuà
A bean, sweetcorn and chick-pea soup from Liguria.

◆Mezzafegato
Unusual raw sausages made from pigs' livers mixed with sugar, pepper, sultanas, pine kernels and orange peel. Grilled and served hot, they are not to everyone's taste.

◆Mimosa
A gateau, made from sponge cake and whipped cream. It is decorated with bright yellow cake crumbs to resemble the strongly scented mimosa flowers found all over the countryside in springtime.

◆◆Minestra maritata
A Neapolitan dish made from green leafy vegetables, such as chard or sprouting-broccoli, cooked with cheese and served in a meat broth, made by boiling offcuts of pork with sausages and salami.

◆◆Minestrone
A thick soup originating in 11th-century Lombardy. Vegetables, beans and salted meats were cooked together in a large cauldron and eaten as a ritual food to bring on rain. Nowadays, cured ham or bacon replace the salted meats, and the vegetables vary from season to season, but minestrone is still basically a thick soup. Pasta or rice is often cooked in it before it is served with grated Parmesan (see recipe on page 97).

◆◆Minestrone di orzo e fagioli
Thick soup made from beans and pearl barley. A regional speciality from Friuli, it is flavoured with chopped ham rind and lard.

◆◆◆Missultitt
A dish made from salted, dried fish. Found around Lake Como, it consists of salted fish, dried in the sun, then grilled and served with oil and vinegar. Delicious, but makes you rather thirsty.

◆◆◆Misticanza
A selection of mixed green leaves, usually picked wild in the countryside, served as a salad. The overall flavour can be rather bitter, so keep to lettuce unless you are adventurous.

◆◆◆Monte Bianco
Mont Blanc. Deliciously sweet cake made by piling whipped cream and meringues on to a flaky pastry base, then covering them with piped chestnut paste to look like Europe's highest mountain, Mont Blanc. Not to be missed if you have a sweet tooth.

◆◆Mortadella
The Italian answer to luncheon meat. It has a slightly stronger flavour and contains peppercorns and pistachio nuts. Delicious sliced thinly and eaten as a filling in a crispy roll; it is quite cheap, too.

◆◆Mostarda
A mixture of fruit pickled in a mustard sauce from Cremona. Excellent with boiled meats.

◆◆◆Mozzarella
A semi-soft cheese. Originally it was made from buffalos' milk in Campania and southern Latium, where water buffalos are still bred. Nowadays, it is also made from a mixture of buffalos' and cows' milk, but the real mozzarella still comes from its region of origin. The

cheese is moulded into spherical shapes with a knot on the top, or into plaits and bite-sized portions called *bocconcini*. Whatever their shape, they must all be kept in their whey or, like the tiny mozzarellas made near Salerno, buried in thick cream!

◆◆Mozzarella in carrozza

Crisp, golden mozzarella 'sandwiches' dipped in egg and fried until golden. A typical Neapolitan dish meaning 'mozzarella in the coach', it makes a pleasant alternative to meat or fish (see recipe on page 108).

N

◆◆Nervetti or nervitt

Calf's foot boiled with vegetables, then served cold, cut into slivers, with raw, sliced onion, black pepper, parsley and olive oil. Borlotti beans can be added if liked. This is a typical dish from Lombardy.

Nocciole

Hazelnuts. These are grown in parts of northern, central and southern Italy, and in late August and September you can see piles of them left to dry in the sun. Try the fresh hazelnuts on sale at the greengrocer's. Dried, they are used to make cakes, chocolates and chocolate spread.

Noci

Walnuts. Sorrento is famous for its walnuts, which have large, smooth, pale brown shells. In their natural state they are

Bland river fish is marinaded

quite dark but are washed to make them look more appetising! Apart from being served as a dessert, they are used to make liqueurs, and chopped and mixed with cream to make a delicious pasta sauce.

◆◆◆Norcina, alla

Sauce made with crumbled sausages, onion and chillies mixed with cream. Traditionally served with RIGATONI and lots of grated Parmesan.

◆◆◆Norma, alla

Named after Bellini's famous opera, this sauce is made from aubergines, tomatoes and basil. A Sicilian speciality.

A–Z GUIDE TO ITALIAN FOOD

O

Olio d'oliva

Olive oil. The main regions producing olive oil are Liguria, Tuscany and Apulia. The quality of the oil depends on the quality of the olives and how they are harvested; they must not be damaged in any way or the oil will be too acidic. The best olive oils are expensive because the olives are hand picked. *Olio extra vergine d'oliva* (extra fine olive oil) comes from the first pressing and is the best for dressings. The farm-produced olive oils are the most genuine and can be bought direct from the farm. This oil has often not been filtered and looks rather cloudy, but has a rich, dark yellowy-green colour. It is excellent simply on crusty bread sprinkled with salt.

Olive

Olives. The small black olives from Gaeta are used for making sauces or seasoned with orange peel and fennel seeds, then served with starters. Large green sweet-tasting olives are sold in paper cones by the roadside. There are smaller, green, bitter tasting olives dressed with garlic, chillies and oregano. Then, there are the stuffed olives you find in your Martini and fried olives from Ascoli Piceno. A selection of small, plump, black or green types can usually be found in all good grocers, where they are sold loose, so you can ask for a mixture and try them all!

♦♦♦Olive ascolane

Large, green olives from Ascoli Piceno, stuffed with a minced meat mixture, dipped in egg and breadcrumbs and fried. In the Marches, they can be found in the FRITTO MISTO.

♦♦♦Orecchiette

'Little ears' of pasta. Still made by hand from an old recipe. In Apulia, their place of origin, they are traditionally served with a sauce made from turnip tops (*cime di rape*) but can also be dressed with a rich RAGÙ.

Origano

Oregano. This herb is found growing wild and is hung in bunches to dry under the arched porchways. It is used generously in many dishes.

♦♦♦Ossobuco alla milanese

Thick marrow-bone veal steaks, cooked in butter and wine with *gremolada*, a mixture of finely chopped garlic, lemon peel and rosemary. A special spoon is used for eating the marrow which is considered a delicacy. A traditional Milanese dish which has become a national favourite, but is often found cooked in tomato sauce nowadays.

P

♦♦♦Pagliata

Pajata, in Roman dialect, this is the milk-filled intestines of a suckling calf, cooked in a spicy tomato sauce and served with *rigatoni*. This delicacy can be found in the *osterie* in Testaccio, an old part of Rome near the slaughterhouse.

♦Pandoro

A large, tall, star-shaped cake, similar to rum baba in texture, dredged with icing sugar. Served at Christmas, it was originally made in Verona but has become a national favourite.

Ancient Trees Bearing Versatile Fruit

The gnarled appearance of many olive trees matches their longevity, for they are expected to live for anything up to 600 to 700 years and there are tales of trees far older.

The fruit-bearing pattern tends to be a good harvest once every two years. Green olives are harvested around September or October. Black olives are the ripened fruit and they are ready for picking from November to December. Fruit destined for oil production is harvested around January.

The method of harvesting may be as important as the quality of the crop, as only hand-picked olives are used to make the finest oils. Mechanical picking involves shaking the olives from the trees.

Freshly picked olives are bitter and the traditional treatment involves soaking the fruit in regular changes of water or brine for up to 15 days. Only then are they ready for pickling in brine or flavouring with herbs and spices, and combining with oil.

The ripened, perfect fruit are pressed to yield their oil – the best, dark and thick, is the first to come from the fruit. This is not acidic but as the fruit is pressed again the oil has a higher acid content and a less pronounced, smooth flavour. Finally, the cheapest, lightest and most acidic of the oils is extracted from the remains of the fruit. Oil from the final pressings has to be purified, sometimes balanced by the addition of an alkali.

Olives, ideal as a take-home gift

Bread and rolls take many forms

◆Panettone
A light, sweet sultana bread which for centuries has been eaten at Christmas. Legend has it that in the 15th century, in the days of Ludovico il Moro, a baker's boy wanting to ingratiate himself with his master, Toni (he wished to marry his daughter!), gave him a special cake recipe. This proved to be a great success when sold as *Pan di Toni*. The name has since been transformed into *panettone* – literally 'large bread'.

◆◆Panforte
Another Christmas speciality, this time from Siena. It is made from candied peel, sultanas and nuts, spiced and packed together so tightly that the cake is difficult to cut but delicious to eat!

◆◆Paniscia
A warming, thick soup made from rice, lard, sausage, cabbage and beans. Served in winter in Valle d'Aosta.

◆◆◆Pappa col pomodoro
A thick Tuscan bread soup with tomatoes and basil. Eaten hot or cold.

◆◆◆Pappardelle
Wide, ribbon-shaped pasta. Traditionally served with rich meat sauces such as hare – *pappardelle al sugo di lepre* is a dish found in Tuscany.

◆◆◆Parmigiano
Parmesan. Probably the most famous Italian cheese. It is the regional name for a type of GRANA.

◆◆◆Passatelli di carne
Freshly made noodles from a mixture of minced chicken, spinach and breadcrumbs, seasoned with nutmeg. They are served in consommé. A regional dish from The Marches.

Passato di . . .
Vegetables or tomatoes turned into purée, either in a blender or by passing them through a sieve.

Pasta
This can be traced back to Sicily in the Middle Ages. It is

now industrially made from durum wheat ground into semolina, mixed with water and forced through nozzles to make different pasta shapes, of which there are over a hundred (see page 56).

◆◆Pasta al forno
Baked pasta. The pasta is mixed with sauce, layered with other ingredients and baked in the oven. The most famous is LASAGNE, but there are also other variations such as RIGATONI mixed with white sauce, chopped ham, mushrooms and peas and sprinkled with breadcrumbs and grated cheese (see recipe on page 101).

Pasta asciutta
Pasta served with a sauce.

◆◆◆Pasta con le sarde
A traditional sardine dish from Sicily. Sardines are layered with pasta, coated with a sauce made from sardines, anchovies, chopped onion, sultanas, pine kernels, the local wild fennel and saffron, then baked in the oven. An unusual mixture which is very tasty and not to be missed when in Sicily.

Pasta e . . .
Usually refers to short pasta shapes, cooked or mixed with vegetables or pulses. They are sometimes referred to as 'thick pasta soups' or *minestre*. Some of the more common are mentioned below.

◆◆◆Pasta e cavolfiori
With cauliflower, olives and capers.

◆◆◆Pasta e ceci
With chick-peas and rosemary.

◆◆◆Pasta e fagioli
With beans, the recipe varying from region to region (see recipe on page 101).

◆◆◆Pasta e lenticchie
With lentils, often flavoured with ham.

◆◆◆Pasta e patate
With potatoes, often flavoured with celery.

◆◆◆Pasta e piselli
With peas flavoured with onions and ham (see recipe on page 106).

◆◆◆Pasta e zucca
With highly peppered pumpkin.

◆◆◆Pasta fresca
Fresh pasta. It is easier than you think to make fresh pasta from flour and eggs. When in Italy, take advantage of the *Pasta Fresca* shops and choose from the many shapes and colours produced. The most common are the ribbon-shaped ones starting with the wide *lasagne*, then *pappardelle*, *fettuccine*, *tagliatelle*, down to the fine *tagliolini*. You can also find fresh coloured pasta – green with spinach, red with tomato and brown with mushroom or truffle. There are also stuffed fresh pastas such as TORTELLINI, RAVIOLI, AGNOLOTTI and CANNELLONI.

◆◆◆Pasta 'ncasciata
A Sicilian savoury baked dish. A tin is lined with aubergines and hard-boiled eggs, then filled with pasta mixed with tomato and basil sauce, chopped salami, diced mozzarella and grated Parmesan. It is baked until golden, then turned out on to a serving dish and sprinkled generously with more grated Parmesan.

A–Z GUIDE TO ITALIAN FOOD

Pasta: Many Shapes, Sizes and Colours

There is an enormous variety of pasta shapes available and new ones are always being manufactured. Spinach, tomato and saffron are just three ingredients which may be used to colour and flavour the dough. Names may change from region to region but most shapes are made both smooth (*liscia*) or ribbed (*rigata*). Some of the more common dried pasta shapes are:

Anellini Small rings. Served in BRODO.

Bucatini Thick SPAGHETTI with a hole running through the centre. Traditionally served with AMATRICIANA sauce in Rome and *stocco* in Naples.

Capellini Fine hairs. The thinnest of the SPAGHETTI family.

Cappelletti Small hats.

Conchiglie Shells. Served with tomato and cream-based sauces.

Ditali Thimbles.

Ditalini Small thimbles. Usually served with thick soups.

Eliche Propellers.

Farfalle Bow ties or butterflies.

Fettuccine Thin ribbons.

Fusilli Spirals. These can be short or as long as spaghetti.

Gnocchetti sardi Small gnocchi-shaped pasta from Sardinia.

Lasagne These wide strips are used for making the famous baked pasta. They can be white or green, smooth or ribbed.

Linguine Narrow tongues. This flat SPAGHETTI is traditionally served with 'pesto' sauce in Genoa.

Lumache Snails. The giant-sized ones are stuffed and baked in the oven while the smaller ones are served with sauces.

Mafaldine These frilly ribbons of pasta are named after the trimmings on Princess Mafalda's dresses. They are traditionally served in the south with RAGÙ (meat) sauce.

Mezze maniche Short sleeves. Short and tubular as their name suggests.

Mista (pasta) Mixed pasta. Different pasta shapes mixed together. Used for making PASTA E FAGIOLI in Naples.

Occhi di lupo Wolves' eyes. Small tubular pasta, similar in shape to DITALI

Orecchiette Small ears. A traditional pasta shape which is still made by hand in Apulia and served with turnip tops or RAGÙ sauce.

Penne Quills.

Perciatelli Another name for BUCATINI.

Pipe Pipes. Similar to LUMACHE in both shape and size.

Rigatoni Large ribbed ones. A short tubular pasta which is always ribbed.

Sedani Celery stalks. These are similar to RIGATONI but smaller and slightly curved.

Spaghetti Thin strings. Now sold in shorter packs but originally had to be broken in half before cooking.

Stelline Small stars. Served in BRODO and a favourite with children.

Tagliatelle Familiar egg noodles. May be green (*verde*) and flavoured with spinach.

Tortiglioni Large twisted ones. These are similar to RIGATONI but are curved and twisted.

Trenette Are similar to LINGUINE

Tubetti Small, short tubes.

Vermicelli Thin worms. These are often called SPAGHETTI even though they are, in fact, slightly fatter. In Naples they are traditionally served with fish sauces.

Ziti Spinsters. This long, tubular, traditional Neapolitan pasta has to be broken into shorter lengths before cooking. It was traditionally served at wedding feasts.

Paste reali
Literally 'royal cakes'. Marzipan is rolled and cut into different shapes, iced and decorated with silver balls. Found in Naples and the south at Christmas.

◆◆Pasticcio di maccheroni
A sweet short-crust pie filled with pasta coated with a rich meat sauce, from Emilia–Romagna. A sweet-sour combination served hot or cold.

◆◆◆Pastiera napoletana
A sweet pastry case filled with sweetened ricotta cheese, egg yolks, candied peel and sweetcorn. It is traditionally served at Easter in Naples and the south. For cheesecake fans.

◆◆◆Pecorino
A hard cheese, made from ewes' milk, found particularly in Latium, Tuscany, Sicily and Sardinia. Look out for the locally made cheeses sold on market stalls or by the roadside. *Pecorino* has a strong, sharp flavour, is delicious with olives and is frequently served grated with pasta.

Penne
Pasta quills.

◆◆Peperonata
Red and yellow peppers fried in olive oil and garlic with onions and tomatoes. Served as a vegetable, it is a delicious (but often highly indigestible) dish.

Peperoncino
Dried red chillies. They are used extensively, both ground and whole. Dried and threaded on to string, they look attractive hung in the kitchen.

A–Z GUIDE TO ITALIAN FOOD

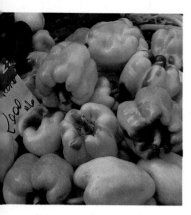

Peppers: try them roasted as a salad (see recipe on page 110)

◆Peperoni ripieni or **imbottiti**
Stuffed peppers. They make a delicious main course in the summer. The filling varies from region to region and can be based on minced meat, tuna or other vegetables such as aubergines. Served hot or cold.

◆◆◆Pescatora, alla
Fisherman's sauce. It contains seafood and shellfish, and is served with tomatoes or without (IN BIANCO). This sauce is often spiced with chilli.

◆◆◆Pesce arrosto
A whole fish, 'roasted' or baked in the oven with a little garlic, parsley, olive oil and wine. It is filleted and 'beheaded' by the waiter. Be careful when ordering it, as the price quoted on menus usually refers to 100g/4oz – the fish is sold by weight, and is usually meant to be eaten by at least two people, depending on size.

◆◆Pesce persico
Perch. When made into a risotto, it is a speciality of the lakeside restaurants around Lake Como.

Pesce spada
Swordfish. These huge fish, with their long pointed 'swords' and their silvery skins, can be seen on the fishmongers' slabs, where they are cut into steaks, ready to be baked or barbecued. A real treat, and no bones to cope with!

◆◆Pesce spada alla ghiotta
Swordfish cooked in a rich tomato sauce flavoured with capers and black olives, from Messina.

◆◆◆Pesce spada alla griglia
Baked or barbecued swordfish.

◆◆◆Pesto genovese
Famous basil sauce from Genoa. Fresh basil leaves, garlic, pine kernels and grated pecorino cheese are chopped and pounded together in a pestle and mortar. Then olive oil is slowly added to make a smooth green paste. It is served with pasta or used to flavour minestrone. Some people now use a blender, but not without feeling guilty (see recipe on page 103).

◆Peverada
A strong-tasting sauce made from chicken livers, anchovy fillets, pickles, parsley and grated cheese, mixed with vinegar and cooked in garlic-flavoured olive oil. Served with poultry in Veneto.

◆Pezzenta
Once a tasty 'poor man's' salami, made from pork offcuts highly seasoned with pepper

and garlic. Now it is enjoyed by rich and poor alike!

◆◆Piadina romagnola
Thin, pizza-like rounds of bread. Found in bars and on roadside stalls, they are heated up, filled with Parma ham and cheese, then folded in half. An excellent snack when touring Romagna.

Piccante
Food spiced with chilli or, in the case of cheese, with a strong flavour.

◆Piccatina al limone
Thin veal escalopes cooked in butter and lemon juice, and sprinkled with chopped parsley. A dish with a really fresh flavour.

◆Pinolata
A type of Madeira cake flavoured with pine kernels. Cut into slices and served with Vin Santo (sweet wine) as a dessert in Tuscany.

Pinoli
Pine kernels. They are found in the cones of the Mediterranean cluster-pines which abound in central and southern Italy. Also sold ready-shelled in small packets, or loose from the grocer's, they are an essential ingredient in PESTO. Expensive, but 100g/4oz go a long way, and they keep well in an airtight jar.

◆Pinzimonio or cazzimperia
A dip made from olive oil, salt and freshly ground black pepper. A selection of raw vegetables, such as celery, spring onions, carrots, radishes and fennel are used for dippers. Deliciously refreshing after a rich meal.

◆◆Piselli al prosciutto
Peas cooked with chopped onion and ham (see recipe on page 106).

◆Pitta
Calabrian name for pizza-pie. It is usually filled with ricotta, sausage and hard-boiled eggs or tuna, tomatoes, black olives and capers. Made from recipes handed down from mother to daughter, *pitta* is rarely found outside the home.

Pizza
Pizzas, as we know them today, originated in Naples in the 18th century. Neapolitan pizza has a higher border and is slightly thicker than the Roman variety. But whatever its origin, a genuine pizza must be cooked in a wood-fired oven, next to the glowing embers.

◆Pizza di Pasqua
A cheese-flavoured bread made with ewes' milk cheese. Originally made only at Easter, it can now be found all year round in Umbria.

◆◆Pizzaiola, alla
Pizza-maker's sauce. Made from slices of beef cooked with tomatoes, garlic and oregano. The meat is then served as the main course (see recipe on page 102).

◆◆◆Pizzelle
Small, fried pizzas. Topped with tomato and basil and sprinkled with Parmesan, they are a Neapolitan favourite. They can also be dipped in sugar to make a sweet (see recipe on page 109).

◆◆◆Pizzoccheri
Ribbon-shaped pasta made from white and buckwheat flour. From the Valtellina, it is cooked with cabbage and potatoes and layered with slices of BITTO cheese and

Traditional Pizza Toppings

An authentic pizza is baked in a wood-fired brick oven

♦♦**Pizza ai funghi** with tomatoes, mozzarella and sliced mushrooms. ˙

♦♦**Pizza alla pescatora** with seafood and tomatoes.

♦♦**Pizza bianca** with olive oil and sea salt. Often served as bread in restaurants.

♦♦♦**Pizza capricciosa** or **quattro stagioni** with mixed ingredients such as tomatoes, mozzarella, ham, mushrooms, pickles, olives and anchovy fillets. Something to suit all 'four seasons' and to satisfy even the most 'capricious' customer!

♦♦♦**Pizza Margherita** was first made by Raffaele Esposito, a Neapolitan *pizzaiuolo* in honour of Queen Margherita. He topped it all with the Italian colours of red (tomatoes), white (mozzarella) and green (fresh basil).

♦♦**Pizza marinara** with black olives, capers, anchovies and tomatoes.

♦♦♦**Pizza napoletana** is the name given in Rome to the topping made from tomatoes, mozzarella and anchovy fillets.

♦♦♦**Pizza romana** is the name given in Naples to the *pizza napoletana* served in Rome!

♦♦**Pizza a taglio** is the favourite Italian take-away. This pizza, sold by the slice, and topped with the usual toppings plus many more, is wrapped in paper and eaten in the street or parcelled up to take home.

grated Parmesan. Coated with melted garlic butter before serving, it makes a delicious one-course meal.

◆◆◆Polenta

Made from maize flour and water, polenta is like a very thick savoury semolina. It is left to cool and cut into slices, then baked or fried. Polenta is served in this way in the north, with game and fish cooked in sauces, as a main course. In central and southern Italy, a more fluid version is served on special wooden plates. The polenta is topped with meat and tomato sauce made with sausages or spare-ribs of pork and sprinkled with grated pecorino cheese. Served as a first course, this also makes a filling one-course meal.

◆◆◆Polenta 'grasa'

Cubes of FONTINA cheese and butter mixed with polenta. When this dish from the Valle d'Aosta is served, everyone helps himself from the pan placed in the centre of the table.

Pollo

Chicken

◆◆Pollo alla Marengo

Chicken pieces served in a wine sauce, topped with croûtons, eggs and prawns. Originally, it was a simple chicken dish offered to an exhausted Napoleon at an inn in Marengo, after his victory over the Austrians.

◆◆Pollo alla romana

Roman style chicken. Cooked with tomatoes, peppers, garlic and wine.

◆◆Pollo arrosto

Freshly barbecued chicken with crisp golden skin,

beautifully seasoned. It can be bought in the *rosticceria* and *pizza a taglio* shops. With roast potatoes, it makes a delicious ready-made meal.

◆Polpette

Meatballs made from minced beef, flavoured with cheese, parsley and onion or garlic. They can either be fried and served as a main course or cooked in tomato sauce. A sweet-sour version can be found in the south, made from minced pork, pine kernels and sultanas.

◆Polpettone

A meat loaf very similar to the POLPETTE.

◆◆◆Polpi affogati

Octopuses which have been 'drowned' in a spicy tomato sauce. This Neapolitan speciality is delicious with spaghetti (see recipe on page 99).

◆◆Polpo all'insalata

A chilled salad made from boiled octopus chopped into small pieces and mixed with garlic, celery, carrot and parsley. It is dressed with olive oil and lemon juice. Served as a starter or summer main dish, this salad is a 'must' for adventurous fish lovers.

Pomodori

Tomatoes. These grow in all shapes and sizes. The small cherry tomato is hung under porchways to provide 'fresh' tomatoes for winter sauces. The plum-shaped San Marzano tomato is canned and exported all over the world. The strange-looking ribbed tomato is ideal for salads or, when too ripe, for stuffing and baking in the oven.

A–Z GUIDE TO ITALIAN FOOD

◆◆◆Pomodori con riso
Tomatoes stuffed with rice and flavoured with garlic, parsley and oregano. Found in the centre and south, they are baked with sliced potatoes which absorb the juices and make a tasty summer lunch.

◆Pomodoro, al
Tomato sauce flavoured either with onion or garlic and basil.

◆◆◆Porceddu
Suckling pig roasted whole on the spit. Basted in its own juices to make the crackling crisp, the meat inside remains tender and succulent. When in the Sardinian countryside you must seek out this traditional dish in local restaurants.

◆◆◆Porchetta
Roast pig, killed at about six or seven months and stuffed with garlic, rosemary, ground black pepper and grated pecorino cheese. It is sliced cold with a little stuffing and a piece of crunchy crackling. *Porchetta* is sold on roadside stalls which also supply the bread. Some also provide a few tables in the shade of the nearest tree, where you can enjoy your *porchetta* with a glass of local wine. Found in central Italy, especially near Rome.

◆◆◆Porcini
Wild edible boletus mushrooms. They appear when the sun is still hot, after a cloudburst. August and September are the ideal months, but unless you are an expert it can be very dangerous to pick your own. Fresh *porcini* are roasted or grilled whole with garlic and parsley. Dried, sliced *porcini* make delicious pasta sauces.

◆Profiteroles
A pile of small choux pastry puffs filled with whipped cream and coated with chocolate sauce. This sweet can be found in most good restaurants, especially in the north.

◆◆◆Prosciutto crudo
Italian cured ham. It is often referred to as Parma ham but there are, in fact, various types. The hams from Parma and Langhirano, for example, are medium-salty and very tasty, having been matured for a minimum of six months. San Daniele, from Friuli, is sweeter and has a more delicate flavour, while the *Prosciutto di montagna*, locally cured 'mountain' hams found in Tuscany, Umbria and Latium, are decidedly saltier and have a stronger flavour; being still on the bone, they are carved by hand. Whichever you choose it must be freshly sliced, if it is not vacuum packed, as it changes its colour and flavour very quickly.

◆◆◆Prosciutto e melone or fichi
Paper-thin slices of PROSCIUTTO CRUDO served with wedges of chilled melon or peeled figs. The slightly salty flavour of the ham is balanced by the sweetness of the fruit. Although a summer starter, it is good served after a plate of pasta.

◆◆Provolone
A cows' milk cheese with a mild (*dolce*) or strong (*piccante*) flavour, depending on its maturity. The huge oblong cheeses are first cut into round slices, then into portions.

♦♦♦Puntarelle

Dark-green, leafy salad vegetable, with thick, fleshy stalks. You can find this vegetable in Rome in wintertime. The stalks are sliced thinly lengthways and dropped into iced water to make them curl. They are then dressed with oil, garlic, crushed anchovy fillets and vinegar. Basketfuls of ready prepared ones can be found at markets for a little extra charge.

♦♦♦Puttanesca, alla

Sauce made with tomatoes, black olives, capers, garlic and anchovy fillets. Often spiced with chillies, and traditionally served with spaghetti and chopped parsley.

Street-corner enterprise

Q

♦Quaglie

Quails. These small game birds are usually grilled. They have a mild flavour, but watch out for the tiny bones.

♦♦Quattro formaggi, ai

Sauce made from four different cheeses mixed with butter and cream.

R

♦♦♦Radicchio

Red-leaved chicory. It has quite a bitter taste. Grown around Treviso in the north, it is served in salads or cut in half, grilled and dressed with olive oil and salt.

♦♦Ragù, al

A rich Neapolitan meat sauce which has been cooked for at least four hours. Generally served with ZITI (traditional Neapolitan pasta), grated Parmesan and sometimes ricotta cheese.

♦Rane

Frogs' legs. Popular in the north where they are often served as part of the FRITTO MISTO.

♦Ravanada

A type of horseradish sauce served with BOLLITO MISTO in Trentino. It is freshly made from horseradish, sugar, vinegar and either grated apple or cream.

♦Ravioli

Probably the best known stuffed, square-shaped pasta. They can be stuffed with fish (*ravioli di magro* found in

Liguria), with aubergines and nuts (*ravioli di melanzane* found in Sardinia) or with meat or ricotta cheese and spinach, like the ravioli found everywhere.

◆◆◆Ribollita
Thick, Tuscan vegetable soup with beans and stale bread. The essential ingredient, however, is the locally grown black cabbage which gives the slightly sour taste.

◆◆Ricciarelli
Small marzipan cakes from Siena, sometimes covered in chocolate. Traditionally eaten at Christmas.

◆◆◆Ricotta
Soft, white, unsalted cheese. *Ricotta romana* is a fresh cheese, originally made from ewes' milk, nowadays often mixed with cows' milk. The name *ricotta* means 'recooked', as it is made from the whey left over from cheese-making, which is reheated. On coagulation, the flakes of cheese are skimmed off, put into small baskets and left to drain until the next day. Look out for the genuine ricotta sold by shepherds.

Rigatoni
A short, ribbed pasta.

◆◆Ris e verz
Rice and cabbage soup from Lombardy. It is served with chopped parsley, ground black pepper and grated Parmesan.

◆◆◆Risi e bisi
Rice and peas. A traditional Venetian dish served with grated Parmesan. Should be tried when in Venice.

Riso
Rice. One of the essential ingredients in Italian cuisine, it is served as RISOTTO, or rice salad, mixed with a sauce, added to soups or made into savoury balls and fried (SUPPLÌ). Grown in Piedmont, Lombardy, Emilia–Romagna and Veneto, it is classified into four categories: *originario*, the smallest grain, *semifino*, *fino* and *superfino*, the longest.

Risotto
A savoury rice dish. Various ingredients are cooked together with rice, stock being added gradually during the cooking until the rice is just cooked. It can be flavoured with vegetables such as mushrooms or artichokes, with fish or shellfish or with meat or sausage.

◆Robiola
A mild, creamy cheese with a reddish rind, made in Lombardy and Piedmont. The best ones come from the pre-alpine valleys of Lombardy, where they are still matured in mountain caves.

◆Rognone trifolato
Calf's kidney, sliced thinly and sautéed in olive oil, wine and onions.

Rosmarino
Rosemary. With its small, needle-like leaves and penetrating perfume, this herb is used to flavour roasts. It can be found fresh at the greengrocer's and dried at the supermarket.

◆◆◆Rughetta
A strong-flavoured, dark green leafy salad vegetable. Either picked wild or grown in allotments, it is excellent mixed with salads and tastes vaguely like watercress.

Risotto: Monarch of Rice Dishes

The exact ingredients may well vary according to the seasons or the mood of the chef but the result is moist and rather creamy. These are the most common combinations.

♦♦♦**Risotto ai funghi** with mushrooms, often PORCINI (see recipe on page 104).

♦♦**Risotto al Barolo** with the famous red Barolo wine.

♦♦**Risotto alla crema di scampi** with cream and prawns or scampi.

♦♦**Risotto alla mantovana** or **alla pilota** with crumbled salami, butter and Parmesan.

♦♦♦**Risotto alla milanese** can be traced back to the 16th century when an unknown painter, working on the Duomo of Milan, fell in love with his master's daughter. At his wedding feast, he served this yellow risotto, coloured with the saffron used in his paints! Since then, this Milanese speciality has been cooked with bone marrow and meat stock and coloured and flavoured with saffron.

♦♦♦**Risotto alla pescatora** with squid, prawns, mussels and clams. Often spiced with chilli.

♦♦**Risotto alla valdostana** with melted Fontina cheese and wine.

♦♦**Risotto al nero di seppie** is flavoured and coloured black with ink sacks from cuttlefish. The fish are also chopped up in the rice.

♦**Rustico**

All savoury pastries and breads are known by this name. Filled with cheese, salami or ham, they are made in the home around Easter, especially in the south.

S

♦♦♦**Salame**

Salami – a highly seasoned sausage made from pork, sometimes mixed with beef. The meat is minced or chopped with pork fat and combined with wine, peppercorns, garlic and spices such as fennel seeds or chillies. This mixture is then forced into tubular bags, made from natural fibres, which are tied at each end and left to marinate in brine before being hung in a cool, dry place to mature. Some are smoked.

Look out for local salami

Each region has its own type of salami. Ask the local butcher if he makes his own: these 'home-made' ones are really tasty.

Salsa
Sauce. Usually refers to the uncooked variety such as mayonnaise.

◆◆Salsicce
Sausage. Italian sausages are very spicy. Nearly every region has its own speciality, but the best ones, like the salami, are made by the village butcher. Best grilled over a wood or charcoal fire, they are often served with beans or a green vegetable which has been sautéed in oil, with garlic and chilli pepper. They are also served in a tomato sauce with pasta or POLENTA. It is difficult to find a *trattoria* without sausages on the menu.

◆◆◆Saltimbocca alla romana
A very tasty Roman dish made from thin veal escalopes flavoured with cured ham and sage, and cooked in butter and wine. It is so good that it 'jumps in your mouth' – the meaning of *saltimbocca* (see recipe on page 106).

Salvia
Sage. Fresh or dried sage can be found at the greengrocer's. The greyish green, velvety leaves of this herb have a strong flavour and should be used sparingly.

◆◆Sanguinaccio
A dense chocolate spread found in the south when pigs are slaughtered. Made from pigs' blood which has been cooked with sugar, chocolate and pieces of candied peel

and flavoured with cinnamon and vanilla, it is eaten with sponge fingers as a sweet. The home-made version is best, but you can also find it at the grocer's.

◆◆Saor
A Venetian sauce made from onions, vinegar, spices, pine kernels and sultanas. It is used for marinating fish.

Sarde
Sardines.

◆◆◆Sarde a 'beccaficu'
Sardines, 'fig-pecker' style. They are boned, stuffed, dipped in flour and beaten egg, then fried with their tails left on so that they resemble the small birds they are named after. The filling varies from town to town: breadcrumbs, cheese and tomatoes in some places, onion, sultanas and pine kernels in others. A symbol of Sicily, they must be tried on a visit to the island.

◆◆◆Sartù di riso
A rice 'pie' from Naples. A 'crust' of rice cooked with a rich RAGÙ sauce is filled with layers of mozzarella, hard-boiled eggs, chicken livers, sliced sausages, peas, mushrooms and more *ragù* sauce. This rich, elaborate dish is becoming increasingly difficult to find.

◆◆◆Sauté di vongole
Fresh clams (VONGOLE) cooked in oil and garlic until their shells open, served with lashings of chopped parsley. Delicious served with fresh, crusty bread as a starter or summer main course.

◆◆Sbrisolona, la
A traditional cake from Mantua which looks and tastes rather

like a 'crumble', with the addition of finely chopped almonds.

◆◆Scaloppine

Escalopes, usually of veal. The thin slices of veal are typically, dipped in seasoned flour and fried in butter or olive oil. *Scaloppine* can be flavoured with lemon juice (*al limone*), white wine (*al vino*), or a sweet, sherry-like wine (*al Marsala*). Easy to prepare, they can be found in most restaurants.

◆◆◆Scamorza

A cows' milk cheese which is similar to mozzarella but is slightly matured. It is often served grilled, when it becomes crusty outside and soft in the centre.

◆◆Sciatt

Little fritters flavoured with BITTO cheese and GRAPPA liqueur and fried in butter or lard. They are served piping hot as a starter. A delicious treat from Valtellina in Lombardy.

◆◆◆Seadas

A light pastry case filled with a mild cheese and served warm, coated with honey. This typical Sardinian dessert is a rather unusual taste experience!

◆◆Seppie coi piselli

Also known as *seppie alla romana*. A traditional Roman dish of cuttlefish cooked in tomato sauce and served with freshly boiled peas.

◆◆◆Sfogliatelle di Santa Rosa

Crispy cakes filled with custard cream. Every year, at the end of July or beginning of August, in Conca dei Marini near Salerno, there is a *festa* in honour of these cakes. Originally made by the

New use for an old olive press

cloistered nuns of St Rose's convent, who offered them to the poor on St Rose's Day.

◆◆◆Sfogliatelle napoletane

Small cakes made either from a type of crisp puff pastry and called *ricce* or from shortcrust and called *frolle*. Both are filled with sweetened ricotta cheese and candied peel, and flavoured with vanilla and cinammon. If you are ever in Naples early in the morning, your nose will lead you to the nearest cake shop taking the first batch of *sfogliatelle* out of the oven. An irresistible mid-morning snack.

◆◆Sgavecio

A Ligurian dish of small fish which have been fried and pickled in vinegar and wine with onions and spices.

◆◆Soffritto
A Neapolitan speciality made from pigs' offal cooked in tomato purée, oil, lard and chilli pepper and flavoured with bay leaves and rosemary. It is served with spaghetti or toast.

◆◆Sopa cauda
Soup made from layers of bread and boned pigeon, covered with broth. Traditionally served in the Veneto in an earthenware pot, it is more like a 'pudding' than a soup!

◆◆Soppressata
Salami made from pig's head and tongue with spices and pistachio nuts. It can be found in most grocers' and butchers' shops in Tuscany. *Soppressata* means 'pressed'. Many more varieties can be found, especially in the south, all called by the same name.

◆◆Sorrentina, alla
Sauce made with tomatoes and basil, from Sorrento. Cubes of

Enjoying a meal al fresco

mozzarella cheese are added when mixing the sauce with the pasta. Served with grated Parmesan.

Spaghetti
Long thin pasta, the word means 'little strings'. Some find this best known of pastas rather difficult to eat. The secret is not to wind too many strands around your fork at once, and then to pop them into your mouth before they have a chance to unwind. Italian etiquette is still undecided whether you can use a spoon to help, or not!

◆◆◆Speck
A smoked cured ham from Alto Adige. It is served as a starter with other cooked meats. Delicious vacuum-packed, home-cured hams can be bought all over the region – a treat for smoked meat fans.

◆Spezzatino
A stew, usually made with

young beef or veal cooked in a tomato sauce. It is served with potatoes and peas. There is also a version without tomatoes, cooked in white wine.

◆Spiedini
Skewers filled with various combinations of meat, fish and vegetables.

Spuntino
Snack.

◆◆◆Stinco di maiale al forno
A whole pork shank, from knee to trotter (not with trotter), per person, roasted in the oven with garlic, rosemary and wine. It is cooked until the meat becomes tender and succulent, while the crackling becomes crisp and crunchy. It is better not to order anything for starters as it is too good to leave on your plate. A speciality from Trentino–Alto Adige.

◆◆◆Stoccafisso
This dried cod is often confused with the salted cod called BACCALÀ. It is imported from Norway. The stiff fish can be seen hanging in grocers' shops or on market stalls. It has to be soaked for several days before it can be cooked. *Stoccafisso* has a very strong flavour – stronger than *baccalà* – and is not to everyone's taste. See also BACALÀ ALLA VICENTINA and BACALÀ MANTECATO.

◆Stracchino
A fresh, creamy, fat cheese made from cows' milk, with a very mild flavour which soon turns bitter when kept too long. Sold in individually wrapped portions, it is ideal for spreading on rolls.

◆Stracciatella
A thin Roman soup made by stirring a mixture of beaten egg and grated cheese into boiling BRODO. It is then served with more grated cheese if liked.

◆◆Stracotto
A joint of lean beef, larded with streaky bacon, and braised with onion, a little tomato purée and wine in an earthenware pot for four hours. Literally translated, *stracotto* means 'overcooked', and the meat is so tender that it melts in your mouth. Served wih potato purée or POLENTA, it is a traditional dish from Lombardy and Emilia–Romagna.

◆◆Strangolapreti
Tiny dumplings made from breadcrumbs, spinach, sultanas and pine kernels. In Trentino, they are served with melted butter and grated cheese. In the south, the curious name of 'priest chokers' refers to GNOCCHI made from flour and water and served with RAGÙ sauce.

◆Strudel
Apple, nut and sultana strudel pastry roll, spiced with cinammon. Can be found all over Trentino–Alto Adige where it is sold whole, or in portions topped with whipped cream.

◆◆Struffoli
A Neapolitan Christmas sweet made from tiny balls of fried pastry covered with honey and decorated with candied peel, glacé cherries and 'hundreds and thousands'.

Sugo
Pasta sauce. There are hundreds of different pasta

sauces; new ones are invented every day. *Aglio, olio, peperoncino* is one of the simplest, containing oil, garlic and chillies (see recipe on page 102). The most common appear alphabetically within the A–Z listing.

◆◆◆Supplì
Deep-fried savoury rice balls. Made from rice cooked in tomato and meat sauce, rolled into egg-shaped balls with mozzarella cheese, dipped in egg and breadcrumbs, then deep fried. A Roman speciality, they make a wonderful filler while waiting for your pizza.

T

◆◆Taleggio
Tasty, ivory-coloured cheese, made in large, flat squares. It was originally made in Val Taleggio but can now be found all over the north. Its flavour resembles Camembert and gets stronger as it matures.

◆◆Taralli
Savoury ring-shaped biscuits from Naples. They are made with pork dripping and lots of ground black pepper. Strands of dough are twisted together, with whole blanched almonds pushed in at random to roast while the biscuits bake. They are delicious as a snack with a glass of chilled wine.

◆Tartine
Canapés with truffle, chicken liver or olive pâté. Served hot or cold as a starter.

◆◆◆Tartufo
White and black truffles. A real delicacy, they grow underground. Armed with torch and trowel, the truffle 'hunter' goes out at night to avoid being seen digging in his 'secret' place, where specially trained dogs have sniffed out a find. The more prestigious white truffle (*tartufo bianco*) from Alba in Piedmont, can grow as big as an orange, and is found in autumn and winter. The black truffle (*tartufo nero*) is found in Umbria. Both have a strong flavour and intense, penetrating perfume, should be used sparingly, and are grated on to risottos, salads and sauces.

Tiella
The local dialect for 'baking tin' in Apulia, where many dishes are layered with potatoes and baked in the oven.

◆◆Tiella di sardine
Tiella made with small sardines (*sarde*). Beaten egg and grated cheese are poured over before the dish is baked until golden.

◆◆◆Tiramisù
A deliciously rich dessert made from sponge fingers soaked in strong black coffee, then layered with brandy-flavoured whipped cream and eggs (see recipe on page 112).

◆◆Tomini
Small individual fresh cheeses made in Piedmont. They have a very delicate flavour and are served with olive oil and ground black pepper as a starter or to end a meal. The adventurous may like to try *tomini elettrici* marinated in oil, vinegar, chopped garlic and chillies.

Tonno
Tuna.
◆◆Tonno, al
Sauce made with tomatoes and tuna, often spiced with chillies. Traditionally served with spaghetti and chopped parsley.
◆◆Tonno e fagioli
Canned tuna mixed with cannellini beans, onion and parsley and dressed with olive oil and vinegar or lemon juice. A delicious snack (see recipe on page 110).
◆Tonno e pomodoro
A salad made from sliced tomatoes, hard-boiled eggs, new potatoes and tuna dressed with ground black pepper and olive oil. A quickly prepared tasty summer snack.
◆Torta di mandorle
Sponge cake filled with apricot jam, moistened with liqueur and covered with piped almond paste. It is one of the most common cakes.
◆◆◆Torta Pasqualina
Puff pastry case filled with either beet tops or artichokes mixed with beaten eggs and cheese. From Liguria, it is served traditionally at Easter.
◆◆◆Tortelli di zucca
An unusual stuffed pasta, filled with sweetened pumpkin, from Mantua. Served with melted butter and grated Parmesan, it is definitely for sweet-and-sour lovers.
◆◆◆Tortellini
Ring-shaped pasta stuffed with a meat mixture. A speciality of Emilia–Romagna, it is served either in BRODO, with melted butter and cheese or with meat sauce. Delicious with cream if you are not counting calories.

◆◆Totani ripieni
A member of the squid family with a slightly sweeter flavour than squid. In Sicily they are stuffed with a savoury breadcrumb mixture and baked on a bed of sliced lemons. In Apulia, they are baked with potatoes, while in Tuscany you will find them stuffed with greens and casseroled with chillies.
◆◆Tozzetti
Small, hard biscuits made with hazelnuts and almonds. Served in Tuscany with a glass of Vin Santo (sweet wine).
Trenette
A type of 'flattened' spaghetti. It is traditionally served with PESTO. Also called *linguine*.
Triglie
Red mullet.
◆◆◆Triglie alla livornese
Red mullet, Leghorn style.

Calabrian fisherman

In this traditional Tuscan dish, the fish are fried in oil and chillies and served in a tomato sauce with chopped parsley.

Trippa

Tripe.

♦♦♦Trippa alla romana

Tripe cooked in a dense tomato and vegetable sauce flavoured with mint and served with lashings of grated pecorino cheese. It can be found in the *osterie* in Rome on Saturdays – tripe day there.

♦♦Trota spaccata

'Split' trout, from Valle d'Aosta. The fish are split in two, dipped in flour and fried in spiced butter. This butter is then used to dress the trout when served with chopped parsley.

U

♦♦Uccelli scappati

Kebabs, called 'flown birds', made with bite-sized pieces of pork, pork liver and sausage, separated from each other by sage leaves. They are browned in butter, sprinkled with wine, cooked until tender and served with POLENTA. Small birds can be cooked in the same way.

V

♦♦♦Vincisgrassi

A pasta dish. One of the oldest dishes from The Marches. It is similar to lasagne except that the meat sauce is made from chicken giblets, minced beef and pork. It is heavily flavoured with marjoram.

♦Vincotto

A delicious spread made by slowly boiling down grape juice until it reaches the consistency of honey. Used for making cakes or spreading on bread, like jam.

♦Vitello tonnato

Thinly sliced veal coated with a tuna mayonnaise flavoured with anchovies and capers. This cold, summer dish, originating from the north, is a fresh-tasting main course for a hot summer evening.

Vongole

Clams. The most common shellfish, sold by the kilo at the fishmonger's. Buy those in the date-stamped net bags: they have been officially checked for disease.

♦♦♦Vongole, alle

Sauce made with clams, with or without tomatoes. Traditionally served with spaghetti and chopped parsley.

W

♦Wurstel

Frankfurter sausages. Made from a mixture of pork and beef, they are very popular served with sauerkraut in the *birrerie* (beer houses), sliced for sandwich fillings and chopped up in rice salads.

Z

♦♦♦Zabaione or **zabaglione**

A kind of cooked syllabub

made by whisking fresh egg yolks with sugar and Marsala (a sweet wine similar to sherry). It is served with sponge fingers as a sweet or 'pick-me-up' (see recipe on page 112).

Zafferano
Saffron. Can be bought in tiny packets from the grocer's. A little goes a very long way. An essential ingredient in RISOTTO ALLA MILANESE.

◆◆◆Zampone
A highly spiced sausage in a bag shaped like a pig's trotter (zampone). It is boiled and served sliced, with lentils, at New Year.

◆◆Zeppole
A type of fried doughnut rolled in cinnamon and sugar, found in the friggitorie (fried food shops) in Naples and the south. Traditionally they are made to celebrate St Joseph's day, when they are topped with custard cream and a sour cherry.

Ziti
A long, tubular pasta. It has to be broken up into shorter lengths before cooking. Traditionally served with Neapolitan RAGÙ.

Zuppa
Soup. Some of the most popular ones are listed below.

◆◆◆Zuppa di cozze
Mussel soup. It is made by cooking mussels in their own juice, then adding tomatoes, oil, garlic and parsley. Served with crusty bread, it makes a wonderful light lunch.

◆◆Zuppa di fagioli
A thick soup made from beans, cooked and flavoured according to regional recipes.

◆◆Zuppa di lenticchie
Thick lentil soup, usually flavoured with ham and served with croûtons.

◆◆◆Zuppa di pesce
Spicy fish soup found on the coast in the south. It is made from a mixture of seafood, shellfish and fish, the essential ingredient being scorpion fish (scorfano), which gives the characteristic flavour. The fish are all cooked with tomatoes, oil, wine, garlic and chilli, then served with croûtons. A deliciously filling one-course meal, but watch out for the bones!

◆◆Zuppa d'orzo
A thick barley and potato soup flavoured with pork and bacon, A warming dish from the Valle d'Aosta.

◆Zuppa inglese
'English soup'. It is in fact a dessert and can be compared to trifle. Sponge cake is soaked in liqueur, layered with custard cream and covered with whipped cream. Found in most restaurants especially in central regions.

◆◆◆Zuppa pavese
A couple of eggs poached in boiling BRODO, which is poured over slices of fried bread. It is served in individual dishes with lashings of grated Parmesan cheese. This typical soup from Lombardy was first offered to King Francis I of France after his defeat at the Battle of Pavia in 1525. A farmer's wife, having only bread and broth to offer the monarch, had the brilliant idea of adding two freshly laid eggs to make a dish fit for a king!

WINES OF ITALY

Italian wines are not as well known internationally as they should be. Until about 20 years ago they were poorly promoted, leaving France to dominate the market. However, in the last decade they have regained lost ground and many of the best wines now prevail over their French counterparts.
To protect the image of their wines, the Italians followed the excellent example of the French *Appellation d'Origine Contrôlée* and, in 1963, introduced the DOC system – *Denominazione di Origine Controllata*. This guarantees the origin and quality of each wine which, once approved, may display DOC on its label. A further guarantee was introduced in 1980 – the DOCG, *Denominazione di Origine Controllata e Garantita*, only given to outstanding wines.
There are, however, some excellent table wines which come into neither category, and the local *vino sfuso*, loose wine sold by the litre, or the *vino della casa* served in jugs in *trattorie*, is often pleasant. The main wines found in each region are listed below. The more interesting ones are described in more detail.

PIEDMONT and VALLE D'AOSTA
Dry red: Barbaresco, Barbera, Barolo, Dolcetto, Gattinara, Grignolino, Nebbiolo.
Dry white: Cortese, Erbaluce, Gavi.
Sparkling: Asti Spumante.

◆◆Asti Spumante DOC
A sparkling wine which is pale to golden yellow, sweet with typical aromatic flavour of Moscato grapes. Best served 'on ice'.
Although some historians attribute the origin of this world-famous wine to Pope Leo X de' Medici (1475–1521), a great *spumante* lover, it was Carlo Gancia in 1850 who officially created it by adopting the French *méthode champenoise* to compete with Champagne.

◆◆Barbaresco DOCG
Garnet red with orange reflections, this 'stern', full-bodied wine is dry and smooth. It is best served at room temperature with roasts and other red meat or game. This so-called twin of Barolo, comes from the borough of Barbaresco, south of Asti. A legend recounts that the inhabitants of the area, during the invasion of the Moors,

Barolo, 'the wine of kings'

plied their oppressors with the local red wine. The 'barbarians' got so drunk that the local people were able to cut their throats while they were asleep. The wine has been called Barbaresco ever since. It must age for at least two years; after three it can be called *Riserva*, after four *Riserva Speciale*, but it should not be kept for more than ten years.

◆◆◆Barolo DOCG

Garnet red with orange reflections, this, like Barbaresco, is a stern, full-bodied wine which is dry and smooth. Best served at room temperature, uncorked at least three hours previously, with roasted red meats, game and rich truffled sauces.

This wine, produced in the area around Barolo, a small village half-way between Turin and Cuneo, was first made in the 19th century in the vineyard of the Marquis of Barolo, still one of the largest producers. Barolo improves with age and is ready for drinking at three years old; after five, it can be called *Riserva*.

◆◆◆Gavi DOC

Pale yellow with a hint of green, this wine is fresh and dry. Best served chilled with starters, salads, fish and poultry and is also excellent as an aperitif.

Also known as *Cortese di Gavi*, it is made from the Cortese grapes which grow to the south of Alessandria. Being one of the best Italian white wines, it is often served at official banquets and on special occasions. Gavi should be drunk before it is two years old; it is also available as a dry *spumante*.

LOMBARDY

Dry red: Oltrepò Pavese, Riviera del Garda Bresciano, San Colombano, Valtellina.

Dry white: Franciacorta, Tocai San Martino della Battaglia, Valcalepio.

◆◆◆Franciacorta DOC

Pale yellow with greenish reflections, this wine tastes dry and agreeably savoury. Best served chilled with fish dishes. Makes an excellent aperitif. The name goes back to medieval times when the land where it was produced was freed from vassallage and called Franca Curtis. It is made mainly in Borgonato di Cortefranca, a medieval hamlet in the province of Brescia.

◆◆Oltrepò Pavese DOC

Ruby red in colour, this is a full-bodied, dry wine. Best served at about 18°C/65°F with boiled meats, stews, hams and salami.

Takes its name from the land 'across the river Po from Pavia', where it is produced. Best drunk when young.

◆◆Valtellina DOC

A ruby red wine which is dry and smooth. Best served at about 18°C/65°F with white meats and poultry. Produced in the Valtellina Valley around Sondrio. Best aged for at least a year.

Valtellina *Superiore*, made in specific areas along the valley, should age for two years.

TRENTINO–ALTO ADIGE
Dry red: Cabernet, Caldaro, Marzemino, Merlot, Pinot Nero.
Dry white: Pinot Bianco, Riesling, Terlano, Traminer Aromatico del Trentino.

◆◆◆Marzemino DOC
Dark ruby red with orange reflections, it is a full-bodied, dry and bitterish wine. Best served at room temperature with POLENTA, RAVIOLI, red and white meats and poultry.
This jewel of Trentino wines is not very well known. Mozart, however, was so impressed that he mentioned it in his opera *Don Giovanni*.

◆◆Riesling DOC
Very pale yellow wine with a greenish tinge. It tastes dry, fruity and agreeably acidulous (or slightly tangy). Best served slightly chilled with fish, crustaceans and starters.
The three similar Riesling wines made from three Riesling vines, *Italico*, *Renano* and *Sylvaner*, are all bottled in the traditional long, slim bottle.

◆◆◆Traminer Aromatico del Trentino DOC
Pale yellow verging on golden, this wine is dry, intense and typically aromatic. Best served slightly chilled with fish soups and seafood.
It has such a characteristic taste and bouquet that, once tasted, it will never be forgotten.

VENETO
Dry red: Bardolino, Cabernet, Colli Euganei, Merlot, Valpolicella.
Dry white: Gambellara, Soave.

Medium-sweet red: Recioto della Valpolicella.
Sweet: Vin Santo di Gambellara.

◆◆◆Recioto della Valpolicella DOC
A garnet red wine with a medium-sweet (*amabile*), warm and smooth taste. Best served with dessert.
Made from the same vines as Valpolicella but using the ripest and sweetest grapes. Once harvested, they are left to dry and sweeten further in the sun before pressing.

◆◆Soave DOC
Pale yellow with a greenish hint, this is a dry harmonious wine with a slight almondy aftertaste. Best served chilled with seafood or egg dishes.
Soave is produced in the province of Verona, and legend has it that Romeo and Juliet were sampling a goblet of local wine together when he muttered '*Soave*!', which Juliet took to be an endearment, '*My sweet*'!, whereas he was simply showing his appreciation of the sweet, soft wine!

◆◆Valpolicella DOC
Ruby red turning to garnet on ageing, this is a full-bodied, dry wine. Best served at room temperature with all meats, game and cheeses.
Ernest Hemingway was so taken by the quality of this

Checking the fermentation

everyday wine that he mentioned it frequently in his book *Across the River and Into the Trees*. It should be drunk within five years.

FRIULI–VENEZIA GIULIA
Dry red: Grave del Friuli, Merlot, Refosco.
Dry white: Collio Goriziano, Pinot Grigio, Tocai, Sauvignon.
Medium-sweet white: Picolit.

◆◆◆Picolit DOC
A pale yellow wine with a medium-sweet or sweet taste, agreeable and delicate. Best served chilled with desserts and strong-flavoured cheeses. This is one of the rarest and most expensive wines on the market, as it is produced in limited quantities, the vine not being very prolific. It is always present at state banquets.

◆◆Pinot Grigio DOC
Golden yellow with coppery reflections, this is a dry, full-bodied wine with a slight aftertaste of bitter almonds. Best served slightly chilled with starters, fish, pasta, risottos and white meats. Pinot Grigio can be found in various parts of the north where it varies slightly from region to region, depending on climatic and geographical conditions.

◆◆Tocai DOC
A bright, pale yellow wine with golden reflections. It tastes dry and aromatic. Best served slightly chilled with starters, and egg and fish dishes. Mixed with bitter Campari, soda water and lemon peel, and served with an olive, it makes an excellent local aperitif called *Spitz*.

LIGURIA
◆◆Cinque Terre DOC
Pale yellow in colour, this is a dry wine, typically aromatic. Best served at about 10°C/50°F with fish dishes such as BURIDDA.

The five villages of the *Cinque Terre* cling like limpets to the rocky cliffs north of La Spezia. The vines are miraculously cultivated on terraces cut into the rock, starting at sea-level and climbing up to 800m/2,600ft. Best drunk within the year, and within a maximum of two years.

EMILIA-ROMAGNA
Dry red: Colli Bolognesi, Gutturnio Colli Piacentini, Sangiovese di Romagna.
Dry white: Bianco di Scandiano, Trebbiano di Romagna.
Sparkling: Lambrusco di Sorbara.

◆◆◆Lambrusco di Sorbara DOC
Ruby red, this wine is dry or medium-sweet (*amabile*) and sparkling. Not to be confused with white and rosé alternatives available back home: this red wine is full of Italian character. Best served at 15°C/60°F when dry, with salami, cured hams, stuffed pastas; cooler when sweet, with desserts.

Lambrusco DOC is naturally sparkling; the table wine often has added gas.

◆◆Sangiovese di Romagna DOC
A ruby red wine with a smooth and dry taste, and an agreeably bitterish aftertaste.

Best served at 18°C/65°F with poultry, white meats and egg dishes.

Christened *Sanguis Jovis* (Blood of Jupiter) by a monk, when asked by a monastery guest for the name of the local wine he found so agreeable, this wine has since been known as *Sangiovese*. Best enjoyed while relatively young, but not before April of the year following its production.

TUSCANY
Dry red: Brunello di Montalcino, Chianti, Morellino di Scansano, Parrina, Vino Nobile di Montepulciano.
Dry white: Bianco di Pitigliano, Bianco Valdinievole, Elba, Galestro, Parrina, Vernaccia di San Gimignano.
Rosato: Rosatello Ruffino.
Sweet: Vin Santo.

◆◆◆Brunello di Montalcino DOCG
Deep ruby red tending to garnet on ageing, this is a smooth, dry and warm wine. Best served between 20° and 22°C/68°–71°F, with roasts, game and liver. The bottle should be uncorked several hours previously and the wine decanted.

This aristocratic wine, revered by connoisseurs, was the first to be granted DOCG status. The time, patience and fond loving care needed in production explains not only the very high quality but also the high price of this wine. It can age for up to 50 years in the right conditions.

◆◆◆Chianti DOCG

Bright ruby red, this is a wine which is dry, sapid (pleasantly characterful), slightly tannic, becoming smoother with age. This is a wine best served at room temperature with roasts, grilled meats, game and salami.

In 1924, the small vineyards making the *Chianti Classico*, in the original Chianti-producing area from south of Florence (Firenze) to north of Siena, formed a *consorzio* (association), with a black cock as their symbol, to protect themselves against imitation. There are another two *consorzi* defending the good name of Chianti made in other areas: Centauro and Putto. Bettino Ricasoli, known as the Iron Baron and one of the fathers of Italian Renaissance, established the proportions of the different grapes used to make the modern Chianti. It is still produced on a large scale by the Ricasoli family at their castle in Brolio. Chianti is best drunk within four years, unless it is *Riserva* when it will last for six.

◆◆Galestro

Very pale greenish yellow wine with a clean, dry and fresh taste. Best served chilled with summer dishes and fish. It also makes an excellent aperitif.

A relatively new table wine which takes its name from the grey *galestro* rock (marl) which is found in the area. Its low alcohol content and 'cheerful' character have met with success.

Wine from the City of Towers

◆◆Vernaccia di San Gimignano DOC

Pale golden yellow, this wine is smooth, dry and slightly bitterish. Best served chilled with starters, fish and seafood. It was the first to be granted the status of DOC and one of the most mentioned wines in history. Pope Paul III Farnese bathed in it; Michelangelo sang its praises; Boccaccio dreamed about streams of it; Saint Catherine of Siena and her fellow sisters used it as medicine; and Dante sent Pope Martin IV to purgatory because of it in his *Divina Commedia*.

UMBRIA
Dry red: Colli del Trasimeno, Colli Perugini.
Dry white: Colli del Trasimeno, Orvieto DOC.

◆◆Orvieto DOC
A pale golden yellow wine with a dry or medium-sweet (*abboccato*) taste. Best served chilled, with fish when dry, or with freshwater fish and egg dishes when *abboccato*.
The medium-sweet wine has a typical bitter-almond flavour and saffron bouquet. The dry wine is produced to satisfy market demand. Both wines are best drunk within two years of production.

THE MARCHES
Dry red: Rosso del Conero, Rosso Piceno.
Dry white: Bianchello del Metauro, Falerio dei Colli Ascolani, Verdicchio dei Castelli di Jesi.

◆◆Rosso del Conero DOC
A ruby red, full-bodied and dry wine. Best served at 18°C/65°F, the bottle having been uncorked two hours before serving, with poultry and casseroled meats.
Takes its name from Mount Conero, the picturesque rocky headland to the south of Ancona. It is a shame that this enjoyable wine is not better known outside its area of production.

◆◆Verdicchio dei Castelli di Jesi DOC
Soft, pale yellow in colour, this dry and harmonious wine has an agreeably bitterish aftertaste. Best served chilled with starters and local fish dishes.
One of the best white wines which takes its name from the greenish-yellow colour of the grapes from which it is made, this is best enjoyed young, while its cousin, the *Verdicchio* from Matelica, will withstand a life of two years.

LATIUM
Dry red: Colle Picchioni 'Vigna del Vassallo', Olevano, Velletri.
Dry white: Est! Est!! Est!!! di Montefiascone, Frascati, Colli Albani, Marino, Velletri.
Sweet: Aleatico di Gradoli, Olevano Rosso.
Spumante: Olevano.

◆◆◆Colle Picchioni 'Vigna del Vassallo'
Bright ruby red with garnet reflections, this wine is dry and smooth with a 'lively character'. Best served at room temperature with roasts of red or white meat.
A relatively new wine produced by a family-run business. It has already received great acclaim from wine connoisseurs at home and abroad, and is considered one of the best red wines in Italy today. Best enjoyed before it reaches the age of eight or ten years, depending on the vintage. The dry white Colle Picchioni *Le Vignole* is worth seeking out, too.

◆◆Est! Est!! Est!!! di Montefiascone DOC
A bright, pale yellow wine which is full-bodied and dry or medium-sweet (*abboccato*).

Best served at around
10°C/50°F with pasta, fried
dishes and fish.
Produced on the shores of
Lake Bolsena, this wine owes
its name to Martin, a young
page, who was sent ahead of
his master to seek out inns
serving good wine. He was so
enthusiastic about the one in
Montefiascone that he wrote
the agreed signal three times
('Est!' indicated the presence
of good wine).

◆◆Frascati DOC
A brilliant pale yellow wine
with a dry and slightly
aromatic taste. Best served
between 9° and
12°C/48°–54°F with starters,
fish, salami, cheeses,
vegetables and Roman cuisine.
Considered the 'wine of
Rome', it is served in typical
litre measures in the *osterie*.
Best enjoyed locally when
young.

ABRUZZO and MOLISE
Dry red: Montepulciano
d'Abruzzo.
Dry white: Trebbiano
d'Abruzzo.

CAMPANIA
Dry red: Capri, Gragnano,
Ischia, Per'è Palummo,
Taurasi.
Dry white: Capri, Fiano di
Avellino, Greco di Tufo,
Ischia.

◆◆◆Greco di Tufo DOC
A pale yellow or golden wine
with dry and harmonious taste.
Best served between 8° and
10°C/46°–50°F with shellfish,
crustaceans and fried fish.
A fresco in Pompeii, has a

poem by a rejected lover
complaining about his partner's
frigidity despite the Greco
wine with which she had been
plied the night before. Best
drunk within five years.

APULIA
Dry red: Brindisi, Cacc'è
Mmitte, Copertino,
Primitivo di Manduria.
Dry white: Locorotondo,
Martina Franca, San Severo.
Rosato: Brindisi, San Severo.
Sweet: Aleatico di Puglia,
Primitivo di Manduria.

◆◆Cacc'è Mmitte DOC
Ruby red, this wine is dry and
harmonious. Best served at
18°–20°C/65°–68°F with
soups, white meats and salami.
The unusual name, literally
translated from the local
dialect, means 'Get it out and

Local Apulian wines

A southern Italian bar

put it in', referring to the inn-keeper who should keep drawing off wine from the barrel and filling ùp your glass. Best enjoyed within three or four years.

BASILICATA

♦♦♦Aglianico del Vulture DOC

Ruby red becoming brick red with age, this wine is dry, harmonious and extremely agreeable. Best served at room temperature, uncorked an hour before, with red meats, roasts, game and lamb. Takes its name from the Aglianico vines which grow on the slopes of the volcano Vulture, which was the epicentre of a disastrous earthquake in 1980. The wine, with its typical bouquet reminiscent of strawberries and raspberries, can be kept for up to 20 years. It is the only wine produced in Basilicata,

but some say that it can be counted among the first ten red wines in Europe.

CALABRIA
Dry red: Cirò, Pollino, Savuto.
Dry white: Greco di Bianco, Melissa.

♦♦♦Cirò DOC
Ruby red tending to orange in colour, this is a warm, harmonious and dry wine. Best served at room temperature with roasted red meats, game and poultry.
Produced around Cirò and Cirò Marina on the Ionian coast, it was offered to winners of the Olympic Games from Magna Graecia (the ancient Greek colonies in southern Italy). More recently, it was offered to the Italian athletes competing in the 1968 Olympics in Mexico City. It should age for at least four years and some vintages can exceed ten.

SICILY
Dry red: Cerasuolo di Vittoria, Corvo.
Dry white: Alcamo, Corvo, Etna, Rapitalà.
Sweet: Malvasia delle Lipari, Marsala, Moscato di Pantelleria.

♦♦Marsala DOC
Dark amber in colour, this is generally a slightly syrupy wine. Best served as an aperitif.
Marsala was originally a normal wine, first shipped to England in 1773. To prevent it turning to vinegar during the long voyage, neat alcohol and

concentrated must were added. The British, in fact, had a monopoly in production of Marsala until Vincenzo Florio decided that enough was enough and opened the first Sicilian winery alongside the British. Now produced in the west of Sicily, there are several types: dry, medium dry, sweet and *all'uovo* (with added egg yolks), often prescribed as a pick-me-up.

◆◆◆Moscato di Pantelleria DOC

From golden to amber in colour, this is a sweet, typically aromatic wine. Best served between 6° and 10°C/42°–50°F with desserts and cakes.
It is produced on the beautiful, remote, volcanic island of Pantelleria in the middle of the Mediterranean, where it is the main source of income. The wine is made from the very sweet Zibibbo grapes, with their characteristic cinnamon flavour. The grapes are left to dry in the sun until they reach a pre-raisin state and then pressed to make the famous Moscato Passito di Pantelleria, sweeter and even more alcoholic, sometimes reaching more than 23 per cent.

SARDINIA

Dry red: Cannonau, Carignano del Sulcis, Girò di Cagliari.
Dry white: Nasco di Cagliari, Nuragus, Vermentino di Gallura, Vernaccia di Oristano.
Sweet: Nasco di Cagliari, Girò di Cagliari.

◆◆Cannonau DOC

Ruby red, turning orangy on ageing, this is a dry to medium-sweet wine with a characteristic flavour. Best served at room temperature with red meats and game. Produced all over Sardinia and reflecting the different geographical and climatic characteristics of the island, its flavour changes slightly from place to place. A wine that is best enjoyed within four or five years.

◆◆◆Vermentino di Gallura DOC

Bright pale yellow with greenish reflections, this is a dry, slightly bitterish wine. Best served chilled as an aperitif or with starters and fish.
This excellent, slightly sparkling wine is considered worthy of drinking with oysters! Should be consumed within two years of production.

◆◆Vernaccia di Oristano DOC

An amber-yellow wine with a dry, harmonious taste and a slight aftertaste of bitter almonds. Best served chilled as an aperitif or with crustaceans, especially crayfish and lobster. Vernaccia is virtually undrinkable until it has aged for at least two years in oak barrels. After ageing for another two years, it is transformed into a dessert wine, similar to sherry. One of the most famous of these is called Sardinian Gold, produced by the wine co-operative in Oristano.

A–Z OF DRINKS

A

Acqua

Water. This is perhaps one of the most useful words to know when sightseeing, as it can be a very thirsty business in the heat! You will be given a glass in the bars with your coffee or ice-cream, and you can find plenty of drinking fountains in most cities and towns.

Acqua non potabile *This is water which is not suitable for drinking. If you see this sign above a tap or fountain, then do not drink the water.*

Acqua brillante

Italian tonic water. Served in small bottles.

Acqua minerale

Mineral water. Italy, thanks to its many spas, produces over 200 brands of mineral water. Most are claimed to have diuretic properties or to help the liver to function better, thus aiding digestion, and some are even recommended for dyspepsia. Most regions of Italy produce their own, found in the local shops and restaurants, while others are manufactured on a national and international scale.

Acqua minerale effervescente naturale

A naturally effervescent mineral water which is pleasantly bubbly. Two of the most famous brands are Ferrarelle and San Pellegrino.

Acqua minerale frizzante

Artificially gassed mineral water, where the bubbles jump out and hit you on the nose! It can sometimes have rather a salty flavour due to the carbon dioxide which is added to make it fizzy. Some of the main brands are Appia, Egeria, Nocera Umbra and San Benedetto.

Acqua minerale naturale

Still, plain or 'flat', mineral water which often does not have any particular taste. Fiuggi, Sangemini, Uliveto and Panna are among the more widely distributed.

◆◆Amaretto di Saronno

One of the most popular sweet liqueurs with an almondy flavour. It is excellent drunk neat, but in the summer is also good 'on the rocks'.

◆◆◆Amaro

Bitter-sweet liqueur made from herbs. This is one of the most characteristic types of Italian liqueur. It is recommended to aid digestion after a big meal. There are hundreds of different variations, as each region has its own, the monks being among the most avid producers. When visiting monasteries, look out for their homemade *amaro* and other liqueurs made from ancient recipes by the monks.

◆◆◆Analcolici

Non-alcoholic drinks. For once, the teetotaller need not ask for the usual tonic water, as Italy offers several of these non-alcoholic drinks as aperitifs.

◆Anice

A dry, aniseed liqueur. Mostly used for 'splicing' black coffee.

◆Anisetta

A strong, sweet aniseed liqueur, similar to the French Marie Brizard.

◆◆◆Aperol
This is the trade name of an orange-coloured, bitter-sweet aperitif made from the essences of rhubarb, CHINA and gentian root. It is usually served with ice and a slice of orange with the rim of the glass dipped in sugar. Aperol is very popular due to its low alcoholic content.

◆Aranciata
Sparkling orangeade. Sold by the glass, bottle or can. A really fruity one is called Oransoda.

B

Bibita
A 'drink' – usually of the soft variety.

◆◆◆Bellini
Spumante (sparkling wine) and peach juice. Originally made in Harry's Bar in Venice, but can now be found bottled.

◆Birra
Beer. Italian beer is similar to the French beer or lager. It is pale and slightly bitter in taste, and sold in bottles and cans. Some bars and restaurants also have draught beer (*alla spina* or *spillata*).

◆◆◆Bitter
A type of non-alcoholic aperitif. At the bar you will be asked whether you want it '*rosso o bianco*' (red or white), as there is now one with no artificial colouring which tastes as good as the original red.

◆◆Brandy
A very palatable spirit distilled from wines. During the Fascist period, when foreign words

Mineral water, a good digestive

were taboo, brandy was known as *Arzente* which, although not strictly Italian, was more acceptable than English or French! Most brandies are of a good quality and are widely drunk within Italy, even though they have never really managed to break into the international market on a very large scale.

C

◆◆◆Caffè
Coffee. Coffee is to the Italians what tea is to the English. It is almost an offence to refuse the proffered cup when visiting friends. Coffee-making in the home, however, is a dying art as today's frenetic rhythm does not allow time for the loving care with which coffee should be made.

Coffee: A Drink of Many Options

Coffee was first introduced to Europe by a 16th-century Venetian ambassador to Turkey, so it is not surprising that it became the national drink of Italy. Coffee is served in many ways and the following are some which you may encounter in addition to familiar CAPPUCCINO and ESPRESSO.

Caffè 'al vetro' is coffee in a glass. It is a Roman fad; some can only drink their coffee when served in a glass!

Caffè corretto has been spliced with a liqueur to give it an extra boost.

Caffè doppio are two servings of coffee in one.

Caffè freddo is iced coffee. A summer favourite which can also be used to make a *cappuccino freddo*.

Caffè Hag (don't pronounce the 'h') is for the caffeine conscious; it is decaffeinated.

Caffè latte is a serving of coffee in a glass of hot, creamy milk.

Caffè lungo, a weaker coffee, where the barman leaves the cup under the coffee machine longer.

Caffè macchiato is 'stained' with a drop of milk.

Caffè Sport is a sweet coffee-flavoured liqueur.

Caffè valdostano, served in the traditional carved wooden bowl or *grolla* which is passed around the table, is a very intoxicating mixture of coffee, wine and GRAPPA. Served in the Valle d'Aosta in winter.

Adding the froth to cappuccino

◆**Camomilla**
Camomile tea. This soothing drink is excellent for calming the nerves.

◆◆**Campari**
Famous aperitif made from a mixture of fruit and herbs. It comes in two varieties, Bitter Campari and Campari Soda, whereas Cordial Campari is served as a liqueur.

◆**Cappuccino**
Frothy milky coffee. Probably the most well-known Italian drink outside Italy, it is served with or without froth (*senza schiuma*) and often topped with a sprinkling of cocoa.

◆◆**Centerbe**
A dry, 70 per cent proof, emerald-green liqueur made from herbs (the name means

100 herbs). It is worth trying, even if only to test your stamina!

◆**China**
(pronounced keena) A bitter-tasting liqueur made from the bark of the Peruvian *cichona* tree. Also served hot in the winter.

◆◆**Chinotto**
Italy's answer to Coke and Pepsi.

◆**Cinzano**
Italian aperitif served with ice and a slice of lemon (see also VERMUT).

◆◆**Cioccolata calda**
A thick, creamy hot chocolate topped with oodles of freshly whipped cream. Served in bars in winter.

◆**Cynar**
(pronounced cheenar) A bitter-tasting aperitif made from artichokes. (*Cynara* is Latin for artichoke.)

D

Digestivo
A liqueur. Taken at the end of a meal, a liqueur is supposed to help the digestion.

Dolcificante
Artificial sweetener. Usually available as an alternative to sugar, at no extra charge.

E

◆◆◆**Espresso**
Highly concentrated black coffee. Served in bars in small, thick-lipped cups, which keep it piping hot, it would seem to be the only thing which keeps some Italians going, judging by their frequent visits to the bar during the day! Connoisseurs, however, say that real coffee is made only in Naples, where it is so dense that you can 'stand your spoon up in it'.

F

◆**Fernet**
Bitter-tasting liqueur made from herbs and spices.

◆◆**Filu Ferru**
Sardinian 'Steel Thread', a dry, 70 per cent proof liqueur only meant for the hardy! The steel thread was used to identify the buried bottles, hidden in the days of prohibition.

◆◆◆**Frullato di frutta**
Fresh fruit milk shake. A meal in itself, especially when made with a *macedonia* (mixed fruit salad).

◆◆**Fuoco dell'Etna**
A Sicilian bright red liqueur. It is just as powerful as the Sardinian FILU FERRU, and as warming as its name, 'Etna's fire', suggests!

G

◆**Gazzosa**
A rather artificial-tasting lemonade. Good for mixing with other drinks such as beer or wine.

◆**Gingerino**
Non-alcoholic aperitif with a slight gingery taste.

◆◆◆**Granita di caffè**
A coffee-flavoured water ice

Shining samples of grappa

piled high with freshly whipped cream. Not to be missed by coffee addicts.

◆◆◆Granita di limone
Freshly squeezed lemon juice made into water ice. Really refreshing in the hot sun.

◆◆◆Grappa
A 50 per cent proof, colourless (golden when aged) spirit, produced mainly in the north of Italy, in Piedmont and Veneto. This famous dry liqueur has been produced in Bassano del Grappa, the 'capital' of the grappa region, since the second half of the 18th century. There, near the famous bridge, the Ponte Degli Alpini, you can visit the Nardini distilleries on the banks of the river Brenta. Grappa can also be bought from family vineyards; if you are lucky, this is often excellent and far better than

some in the shops. The famous Nonino grappa can be identified by its characteristic bottles, reminiscent of the chemistry flasks in school laboratories. Some varieties contain a pear or bunch of grapes (how do they get in there?), but the grappa, although fruit-flavoured, is still dry. A sweeter version is made by adding sugar and fruit, such as wild raspberries, redcurrants or the bilberries which are used to make the Mirtillo liqueur found in the Dolomites.

◆◆◆Grattachecca
Crushed ice sprinkled with a fruit flavoured syrup. The *grattachecca* stalls, however, are seen very rarely nowadays but you may be lucky enough to find one at a local fair or seaside resort.

L

Latte
Milk. Italian milk is not as creamy as British. It is sold in half-litre and litre cartons and can also be bought partially skimmed (*parzialmente scremato*) or skimmed (*scremato*). The bars usually serve 'whole' milk, however, either hot (*latte caldo*), tepid (*latte tiepido*) or cold (*latte freddo*).

◆◆Latte di mandorla
Almond milk. It is either diluted with water or mixed with other drinks and cocktails.

◆Latte macchiato
'Stained' milk, coloured with a dash of coffee.

◆**Limonata**
Fizzy lemonade. There is a really fruity one called Lemonsoda which tastes like the real thing.

Liquore
Liqueur. Should you be fortunate enough to be invited into an Italian home, especially in the south, you could be offered the 'family speciality', made from a recipe handed down from father to son. Home-made liqueurs are prepared for special occasions like Christmas or Easter. They are made from ingredients such as orange, lemon or tangerine peel, cherry stones, walnuts or anything else which may take the maker's fancy and is in the family tradition!

M

◆◆**Mandarinetto**
Sweet orange-flavoured liqueur. Used to give a boost to fresh fruit salad. Even better, it is heated up on a really cold day and served as a hot punch sipped through a straw; they say it works wonders with the common cold!

◆**Martini**
Probably the best known of the Italian aperitifs in all three versions: dry, sweet (bianco) and rosso (see also VERMUT).

N

◆◆**Nocillo**
A medium-sweet liqueur made from walnuts.

O

◆◆**Orzata**
A sweet but refreshing almond-flavoured barley water.

P

◆◆◆**Punch**
(pronounced 'ponch') An orange-flavoured liqueur served hot in the winter.

◆◆**Punt e Mes**
One of the oldest vermouths. So-called because it was served in the bar next to the Stock Exchange in Turin, where the customers were always boasting, in local dialect, that their shares had risen a *punt e mes* (one and a half points).

R

◆**Rabarbaro**
A bitter-tasting aperitif made from rhubarb – although you would not recognise it.

S

◆◆◆**Sambuca**
A syrupy sweet aniseed liqueur. Traditionally served in Roman *trattorie* with a *mosca* (fly) floating on the top in the form of a toasted coffee bean. Sometimes it is served 'flambé' by setting light to it in the glass.

A–Z OF DRINKS

◆Sciroppo di ...
Sweet syrups flavoured with fruits such as orange (*arancio*), sour cherries (*amarene*), tamarind (*tamarindo*), lime (*cedrata*) or mint (*menta*). They are diluted with mineral water to make drinks.

Seltz
Similar to soda water. Added to whisky or brandy.

◆◆◆Spremuta di arancio, limone e pompelmo
The freshly squeezed juices of oranges, lemons and grapefruit.

◆◆Strega
(meaning 'witch') Bright yellow lemon-flavoured liqueur sold in a tall bottle with an embossed sun. Around Christmas, you can find delicious Strega-filled chocolates.

◆Succhi di frutta
Italian sweetened fruit juices. They come in small bottles and in the three main flavours of peach (*pesca*), pear (*pera*) and apricot (*albicocca*). They have always been a favourite with children as they are sweeter and thicker than the citrus juices, which have been introduced to satisfy tourist demand.

T

◆Tè or Thè
Tea. Served with lemon, unless you specifically ask for milk (*al latte*).

◆◆Tropical
A summer drink made from almond milk mixed with mint syrup. Very sweet but refreshing.

V

◆Vermut
Vermouth. An aperitif made from wine and herbs. First made and bottled in Turin in 1786 by Signor Carpano, who founded the first distillery. Some vermouths, such as MARTINI and CINZANO, have become world famous, but there are lesser known ones made locally and called simply *Vermut*.

◆◆◆Vino
Wine. Wine can be white (*bianco*), red (*rosso*) or rosé (*rosato*) and dry (*secco*), medium-sweet (*amabile* or *abboccato*), sweet (*dolce*) and sparkling (*frizzante*). See chapter **Wines of Italy** for detailed information.

◆◆Vov
A sweet, thick, yellow-coloured liqueur made from egg yolks, sugar and alcohol. It is an excellent pick-me-up when you are feeling rather fragile!

Z

Zucchero
Sugar. Sugar and artificial sweeteners are usually available on bar counters. However, in the south of Italy you will need to learn the phrase '*Senza zucchero, per favore*' if you prefer no sugar, as southern Italians tend to sweeten everything before serving and you will find drinks exceedingly sweet!

SHOPPING

In this and later chapters, words and phrases are included to help you deal with everyday situations. Phonetic pronunciation guides are given, but for more information on pronouncing Italian see **Language** page 125.

Opening Hours

Each region in Italy has its own laws governing the opening hours of the local shops. As a general rule, however, the food shops open early in the morning around 07.00 or 08.00 hours and close for lunch at 13.00 or 13.30 hours (in the north they close earlier, at 12.00 or 12.30 hours). They reopen after the afternoon siesta at around 15.00 hours in the north and 16.30 to 17.00 hours in the centre and south. They then close in the early evening at 19.00 or 19.30 hours (earlier in the north).
The half-day closing varies from region to region but is usually Wednesday or Thursday, sometimes changing to Saturday afternoons in the summer months. The butchers' shops in some regions close on a different day to the rest, depending on local meat deliveries. In most tourist resorts, however, at the height of the season, you usually find that the shops are open every day, including Sundays. Supermarkets are often open all day in the big cities, or only close for an hour in mid-afternoon. Markets are open only in the mornings, unless a *festa* is coming up, when they

It is always best to ask about local opening times on arriving in a new town:
What time do the shops close?
>A che ora chiudono i negozi?
>*a ke Ora kyOO-do-no ee ne-gO-tsi*

What time do they open in the afternoon?
>A che ora aprono il pomeriggio?
>*a ke Ora A-pro-no il po-me-erEE-jo*

Are they open on Sundays?
>Sono aperti la domenica?
>*sono a-pAir-ti la do-mE-ni-ca*

will stay open through to the early evening on the day before. Cake shops stay open until later in the evening, without closing in the afternoon. They are always open on Sundays, their busiest day, as it is the custom in Italy, when invited home for a meal, to take a present of flowers, chocolates, wine or cakes. They usually close for the day on a Monday or Tuesday. Below is a guide to the main types of food shops, the service they offer, what you can buy and when it is in season.

GROCERS' SHOPS
Alimentari/Salumeria/Salsam-enteria/Pizzicheria/Norcineria
The grocers' shops look very colourful and inviting with their Parma hams, salami and sausages strung from the ceiling, their huge rounds of Parmesan cheese stacked on the shelves, their baskets of

stiff, dried cod and their glass-fronted counters crammed with local cheeses and cured meats, the green and black olives and the enormous cans of tuna fish and salted anchovies. You may find your local grocer's shop sign says 'Alimentari' (from *Alimenti* – foodstuffs), 'Salumeria' or 'Salsamenteria' (referring to the pork products sold), 'Pizzicheria' (from *cose pizzicanti* – things to whet the appetite) or 'Norcineria' (from the town of Norcia, home of pork butchers).

The friendly atmosphere enables you to buy just what you want; one slice of cooked ham, or 100g/4oz of cheese. The law requires the food to be weighed in or on its wrapping paper, but do not worry, the scales allow for this.

Groceries

bacon pancetta *pan-chEt-ta*
bread pane *pAh-ne*
butter burro *bOOr-ro*
cheese formaggio *form-Aj-jo*
coffee caffè *caf-fE*
cooked ham prosciutto cotto *pro-shOOt-to cOt-to*
cured ham prosciutto crudo *pro-shOOt-to-crOO-do*
eggs uova *wO-va*
flour farina *fa-rEE-na*
honey miele *myE-le*
jam marmellata *mar-mel-lA-ta*
margarine margarina *ma-ga-rEE-na*
milk latte *lAt-te*
mineral water acqua minerale *Ac-kwa mi-ne-rA-le*
pepper pepe *pE-pe*
salt sale *sAh-le*
sugar zucchero *dzOO-ke-ro*
tea tè *tEh*

GREENGROCERS' SHOPS
Frutteria/Frutta e Verdura/Ortaggi

Most greengrocers' shops have a display outside the shop, even if it is only two or three crates of fruit (*frutta*) or vegetables (*verdura* or *ortaggi*). Some of them, however, have a wonderful terraced arrangement of all their produce, which is so tempting that it is difficult to choose. Everything should be priced, the prices referring to the cost per kilo, unless otherwise stated: ready prepared mixed salad or MINESTRONE for example, are sold by the *etto* (100g/4oz). There will often be piles of brown paper bags or small baskets lying around for you to serve yourself before handing everything over to the greengrocer for weighing. Some, however, do not like you to touch, especially when the soft fruits are in season. Ask first unless you see others already choosing their own.

Fruit and Vegetables

Available all year round:
apples mele *mEh-le*
aubergines melenzane *me-len-tsAh-ne*
bananas banane *ba-nAh-ne*
cabbage cavolo *cA-vo-lo*
carrots carote *ca-rO-te*
celery sedano *se-dA-no*
chard bietola *byE-to-la*
chilli (dried red) peperoncino *pe-pe-ron-chEE-no*
courgettes zucchini *dzoo-kEe-ni*
garlic aglio *Al-lio*
lettuce lattuga *lat-tOO-ga*
mixed salad insalata mista *in-sa-lA-ta mEE-sta*

mixed **vegetables** minestrone
mi-nes-trOh-ne
onions cipolle *chi-pOl-le*
parsley prezzemolo
pre-tsE-mo-lo
pears pere *pEh-re*
peppers peperoni *pe-pe-rO-ni*
pineapple ananas *a-na-nAs*
potatoes patate *pa-tAh-te*
rosemary rosmarino
roz-ma-rEE-no
sage salvia *sAl-vya*
tomatoes pomodori
po-mo-dO-ri

Best in wintertime:
artichokes carciofi *car-chO-fi*
broccoli broccoli *brOc-co-li*
chestnuts castagne *ca-stA-nye*
cauliflower cavolfiore
ca-vol-fyO-re
fennel finocchio *fi-nOc-kyo*
hazelnuts nocciole *no-chyO-le*
kiwi kiwi *kiwi*
mandarins mandaranci
man-dar-An-chi
oranges arance *a-rAn-che*
spinach spinaci *spi-nA-chi*
tangerines mandarini
man-dar-EE-ni
turnip tops broccoletti
broc-co-lEt-ti
vegetables verdura
ver-dOO-ra
walnuts noci *nO-chi*

Best in the summer:
apricots albicocche
al-bi-cOk-ke
basil basilico *ba-zEE-li-co*
blackberries more *mOh-re*
cherries ciliege *chi-lyEh-je*

figs fichi *fEE-ki*
grapes uva *OOva*
melon melone *me-lO-ne*
peaches pesche *pEs-ke*
persimmons cachi *cA-ki*
raspberries lamponi *lam-pO-ni*
redcurrants ribes (rossi)
rEE-bes (ros-si)
strawberries fragole *frA-go-le*
water-melon anguria
an-gOO-ria
wild strawberries fragoline
fra-go-lEE-ne

BUTCHERS' SHOPS
Macelleria/Beccheria/
Carnizzeria
Most butchers' shops in towns
and cities have an excellent
display of large cuts of meat in
their refrigerated counters.
You must indicate your choice,
how much you need and
whether you want it sliced
thinly or thickly, cut into
chunks, left as a joint, pounded
thin or minced. Some butchers
sell ready-prepared items,
such as kebabs, hamburgers
and breadcrumbed veal
cutlets but these are more
readily obtainable at the
supermarket. If you tell the
butcher which dish you are
planning to make, he will give
you a suitable cut or suggest
another with the meat available.
A *macelleria equina*, by the
way, is a horse meat shop!

Nectarines, a taste of summer

A critical eye in the fish market

Meat, Poultry and Game
baby goat capretto *ca-prEt-to*
beef manzo *mAn-tso*
brains cervella *cher-vEl-la*
chicken pollo *pOl-lo*
chicken breast petto di pollo
  pEt-to di pOl-lo
game cacciagione
  ca-cha-jOh-ne
guinea fowl faraona *fa-ra-Ona*
hare lepre *lE-pre*
kidneys rognoni *ro-nyO-ni*
lamb agnello/abbacchio
  a-nYEl-lo/ab-bAc-kio
liver fegato *fE-ga-to*
meat carne *cAr-ne*
minced meat carne macinata
  cAr-ne machi-nA-ta
mutton montone/castrato
  mon-tOh-ne/ca-strA-to
offal frattaglie *frat-tAl-lye*
partridge pernice *per-nEE-che*
pheasant fagiano *fa-jA-no*
pork maiale *ma-yA-le*
quail quaglia *quAh-lia*
rabbit coniglio *co-nEE-lio*

sausages salsicce *sal-sEE-che*
turkey tacchino *tac-kEE-no*
veal vitello *vi-tEl-lo*
venison capriolo/cervo
  ca-pri-O-lo/chEr-vo
wild boar cinghiale
  chin-ghiAh-le
young beef vitellone
  vi-tel-lOh-ne

FISHMONGERS' SHOPS
Pescheria
The fishmonger's marble slab,
garnished with large green
leaves, is laden with all types
of fish, seafood and shellfish.
The fish to be baked or grilled
are weighed and sold whole
but, if asked, the fishmonger
will clean and descale them
for you at no extra charge. The
larger fish, such as swordfish
or tuna, are sliced into 'steaks',
and some fish, such as cod,
are sometimes filleted. Get
them to clean your octopus
and squid, too, unless you are
feeling adventurous. Shellfish
is sold by the kilo; the clams
come in nets which are date
stamped. If any of the fish has
been defrosted, a notice
should say so, otherwise it
should all be freshly caught.

Fish and Shellfish
anchovies alici *a-lEE-chi*
bass spigola *spEE-go-la*
carp carpa *cAr-pa*
clams vongole *vOn-go-le*
cod merluzzo *mair-lOOt-tso*
crab granchio *grAn-kio*
crayfish aragosta *ara-gOs-ta*
cuttlefish seppia *sEp-pia*
eel anguilla *an-guEEl-la*
fish pesce *pE-she*
grey mullet cefalo *chE-fa-lo*
grouper cernia *chAIr-nia*
king prawns mazzancolle
  mat-tsan-cOl-le

lobster astice *As-tee-che*
mackerel sgombro/maccarello
  sgOm-bro/mac-ka-rEl-lo
mussels cozze *cOt-tse*
octopus polpo *pOl-po*
oysters ostriche *Os-tri-ke*
perch pesce persico
  pE-she pAIr-si-co
pike luccio *lOOt-cho*
prawns gamberi *gAm-be-ri*
red mullet triglie *trEE-lyeh*
salmon salmone *sal-mO-ne*
sardines sarde *sAr-de*
scampi scampi *scAm-pi*
shellfish frutti di mare
  frOOt-ti di mAh-re
sole sogliola *sO-lyo-la*
squid calamari *ca-la-mA-ri*
swordfish pesce spada
  pE-she spA-da
trout trota *trO-ta*
tunny/tuna tonno *tOn-no*
white bream sarago *sA-ra-go*

BAKERS' SHOPS
Panificio/Fornaio/Forno/
Vapoforno/Panetteria
Each region has its own type of
bread made into variously
shaped loaves or rolls. You
can also find home-made
croissants, biscuits and cakes.
Bread is bought directly from
the 'oven' in small towns and
villages. In large cities it is
sold in grocer's or 'speciality
bread' shops. Bread is
weighed and sold by the kilo.

Bread
bread pane *pAh-ne*
French loaf filone filoncino
  sfilatino *fi-lO-ne*
  fi-lon-chEE-no sfi-la-tEE-no
rolls panini *pa-nEE-ni*

CAKE SHOP
Pasticceria
Cakes are often sold in bars,
and cake shops often have a

counter for serving drinks.
They sell chocolates and sweets
as well as large and small
cakes and pastries, ice-cream
cakes and ice-cream. Large
cakes are weighed and sold
by the kilo. Small cakes are
sold individually; they can be
eaten on the spot or taken away.

Cakes, Biscuits, Ice-cream and Confectionery
biscuits biscotti *bis-cOt-ti*
box of . . . scatola di . . .
  scA-to-la di . . .
chocolate cioccolata
  choc-ko-lA-ta
chocolates cioccolatini
  choc-ko-la-tEE-ni
ice-cream gelato *jeh-lA-to*
large cake torta *tOr-ta*
small cakes paste *pAs-te*
sweets caramelle *ca-ra-mEl-le*

DAIRY
Latteria
Most supermarkets and
grocers sell milk and dairy
products, but bars often
display the sign *Latteria*, too.
They sell not only milk but
cream, yoghurt and butter.

VILLAGE STORE
Generi Diversi/Emporio
In small villages, these will
often be the only shop for
miles around. They sell
everything from shoe laces to
pork chops!

MARKET
Mercato
Open-air markets, with their
wooden stands and huge sun
canopies, appear early in the
morning in the streets and
squares of most cities and
towns, then pack up their stalls
around lunchtime. There are

SHOPPING

Seasonal produce in the market

also permanent covered markets in most neighbourhoods. Smaller villages have travelling markets which visit one day a week. They are all usually excellent for both value and freshness. There is a feeling of bustle and activity, with the stallholders crying out their wares in local dialect. The fruit and vegetables are a wonderful sight. Whatever is in season is heaped on to stalls and arranged so temptingly that you usually buy far more than you intended!

STREET STALL
Bancarella
Found along the roadside, often rigged up in the back of a lorry, they often sell just one item – whatever happens to be in season, such as strawberries or artichokes.

FROZEN FOODS
Surgelati
These stores specialise in everything frozen, from cuts of meat and whole fish down to ice-cream. You will not find complete ready-made frozen meals, however.

Useful phrases for shopping
Good morning. Can I help you? What would you like?
    Buon giorno. Desidera?
    bwon jOr-no. de-zI-de-ra
Which one?
    Quale?
    quAh-le
This one/That one *(indicating)*
    Questo/Quello.
    quEs-to/quEl-lo
Here you are! Anything else?
    Tenga! Altro?
    tEn-ga Al-tro
No thank you. How much is it?
    No, grazie. Quant'è?
    no grA-tsieh quant Eh
At the cash desk, please.
    Alla cassa per favore.
    al-la cAs-sa pair fa-vO-re
Thank you. Good day.
    Grazie. Buon giorno.
    grA-tsieh. bwon jOrno

Other useful phrases:
How much does .... cost?
    Quanto costa ......?
    quAn-to cOs-ta .....
Have you any .....?
    Avete del .....?
    a-vEh-te del .....
How much does .... weigh?
    Quanto pesa ..... ?
    quAn-to pEh-sa .....
May I help/serve myself?
    Posso fare da me?
    pOs-so fAh-re da mEh
Is it fresh?
    E' fresco?
    Eh frEs-co

RECIPES

Here are a few recipes for you to 'cook Italian' while on holiday or to try out back home. The easily made dishes are marked * and the more time-consuming ones are marked **. It would be worthwhile looking to see whether you could buy some of the essential ingredients while you are in the country.

Bruschetta con pomodori*

Garlic bread with Tomatoes

Serves 4

This garlic bread can also be served with sliced ham.

4 medium-ripe tomatoes, finely chopped
8–10 fresh basil leaves
4 tablespoons olive oil
salt
4 large thick slices crusty bread
1 clove garlic

Place the tomatoes in a bowl. Wash and pat dry the basil leaves, discarding the stalks. Tear the leaves into small pieces and add them to the tomatoes with the olive oil. Add salt to taste.
Toast the bread over a wood/charcoal fire (or under the grill) until browned on both sides. Half-peel the garlic and rub it over one side of each piece of toast. Cut the slices of toast in half and top each piece with the tomato mixture. Serve immediately.

Minestrone*

Thick Vegetable Soup

Serves 4

Tastier when made the day, or morning, before.

1 thick slice lean 'streaky' bacon
1 large clove garlic, skinned
olive oil
500g/1lb roughly chopped mixed vegetables, such as carrots, celery, leeks, cabbage, cauliflower, courgettes, spinach, broccoli
2 ripe tomatoes, roughly chopped
2 medium potatoes, peeled and diced
salt
100g/3½oz *tubetti* (small, short pasta tubes)
75g/3oz Parmesan cheese, grated, to serve

Chop the bacon into small pieces. Cut the garlic clove into 3 to 4 pieces. Coat the bottom of a deep, thick-bottomed saucepan with olive oil, add the garlic and bacon and fry until the garlic is golden and the bacon crisp. Add all the chopped vegetables. Cover with water, add salt to taste and simmer for about 40 minutes until the vegetables have become a thickish soup. Add a little water to prevent the soup from becoming too thick while cooking the pasta. Bring back to the boil, add the pasta and cook until it is *al dente*. Serve the soup in individual bowls with grated Parmesan cheese.

Antipasto all'italiana*

Italian-style Starter

Serves 4 as a light meal,
6–8 as a starter

8 anchovy fillets (1 small can)
4 individual portions butter
100g/3½oz green olives
200g/7oz thinly sliced cured
  ham (prosciutto crudo)
200g/7oz sliced mixed salami
1 small jar mixed pickles
4 small wild boar sausages
  (salsicce di cinghiale)

Drain the oil from the anchovy
fillets and roll up each one.
Cut the portions of butter into
halves and top each with an
anchovy roll. Arrange the
sliced meats attractively on a
platter, putting the olives,
pickles, sausages and
anchovies in the middle (or
make individual arrangements
on plates). Serve with crusty
bread or breadsticks.

Antipasto all'italiana

Impepata di cozze*

Peppered Mussels

Serves 4 as a light meal,
6–8 as a starter

*This is obviously best made
with mussels you have just
caught yourself! However,
fresh mussels are readily
available from all fishmongers
in Italy. This recipe is not
suitable for frozen or bottled
ones.*

1.5kg/3lb fresh mussels
freshly ground black pepper
2 large lemons

Clean the mussels really well
by putting them in a large bowl
or bucket of water (seawater if
available) and rubbing the
shells together to remove
seaweed or other foreign
bodies encrusted on them. Pull
away the beard or seaweed-
like strands from each mussel
and discard. Rinse well and
place in a large covered pan

over a high heat, tossing them frequently until the shells have all opened. Do not leave them over the heat longer than necessary or the mussels will overcook. Discard any mussels that do not open.

Using a draining spoon, place all the mussels in a large serving bowl. Filter the cooking liquor if necessary to remove any sand, then pour it hot over the mussels. Sprinkle very generously with the black pepper and serve with wedges of lemon and chunks of crusty bread. Use the shells to eat the mussels, scooping up a little juice with each, and squeezing a little lemon on to the mussel before eating.

the ink sacks (be careful of the ink). Remove the eyes and hard 'beaks' in the middle of the tentacles. Rinse well, making sure that there is no sand stuck to the suction pads. Liquidise or crush the tomatoes and slice the garlic cloves. Coat the base of a deep frying pan with olive oil, add the chilli, crushing it to release the flavour. Add the garlic and fry until golden. Add the octopus, cover and cook, turning it occasionally, until tender (about 30 minutes). Add the tomatoes and cook for a further 10–15 minutes until the sauce becomes thick. Taste for salt, but it is not usually needed. Serve sprinkled generously with chopped parsley.

*Polpi affogati***

Drowned Octopus

Serves 4

This dish is well worth the effort if you have been snorkelling and happen to have caught your own octopus. Otherwise, it can be made – even with frozen ingredients – back home.

4 small octopus, about 200g/7oz each
1 (400g/14oz) can plum tomatoes
2 cloves garlic, skinned
olive oil
1 hot chilli
1 tablespoon fresh parsley, roughly chopped

To clean the octopus, turn the heads inside out and remove

Cooking Pasta

Pasta should always be cooked by dropping it into plenty of fast-boiling salted water. Test it two or three minutes before the end of the recommended cooking time. It is perfectly cooked when the uncooked core in the centre is just about to disappear or, in the case of spaghetti, when you can squeeze it between your thumb and forefinger to break it. This state is called *al dente* which means 'resistant to the tooth'. The pasta must then be drained immediately and mixed with the sauce. (If not using a tomato-based sauce, keep a little of the pasta water for mixing, if liquid is needed.)

RECIPES

*Bucatini all'amatriciana**

Bucatini Amatrice style

Serves 4

Amatrice, which gives its name to this sauce, is a small mountain town about 60km (37 miles) northeast of Rome.

1 (400g/14oz) can finely chopped plum tomatoes
olive oil
1 small chilli
1 small onion, skinned and finely chopped
2 thick slices lean streaky bacon (*pancetta*)
2 teaspoons concentrated tomato purée
salt
400g/14oz *bucatini*
75g/3oz pecorino cheese, grated

Bucatini *are thick spaghetti*

Liquidise the tomatoes or crush them with a fork. Coat the base of a deep heavy-based frying pan with olive oil. Add the chilli crushing it to release its flavour. Add the onion and bacon and fry until the onion is transparent and the bacon crisp. Add the tomato purée, tomatoes and salt to taste, and cook over a low heat, stirring occasionally, for about 30 minutes until the sauce becomes thick.
Meanwhile, bring a pan of salted water to the boil for the *bucatini* and cook the pasta so that it is ready at the same time as the sauce. Drain the pasta well, transfer to a warmed serving dish and mix with half the grated cheese and the sauce. Serve, with the rest of the grated cheese to be added as desired.

*Pasta al forno***

Baked Pasta

Serves 4

*Half-litre cartons of white
sauce (béchamel) can be
bought in most Italian grocers'
shops and supermarkets.*

100g/3½oz butter or
   margarine
200g/7oz mushrooms, thinly
   sliced
1 clove garlic, skinned
200g/7oz small frozen peas
2 thick slices lean cooked
   ham, chopped, fat removed
300g/10oz *rigatoni*
0.5litre/1pint pouring white
   sauce (béchamel)
100g/3½oz Parmesan cheese,
   grated
salt and pepper

Melt a third of the butter in a
pan and fry the mushrooms
with the garlic clove. Remove
the garlic and discard. Cook
the peas in boiling salted
water. Drain and add to the
mushrooms with the ham. Cook
the *rigatoni* in a pan of boiling
salted water until three-
quarters cooked, then drain.
Set the oven at 200°C, 400°F,
gas 6. Heat the white sauce,
add half the grated cheese
and another third of the butter.
Mix two-thirds of the sauce
with the *rigatoni*. Layer the
rigatoni with the peas, ham and
mushrooms in an ovenproof
dish (or disposable foil baking
tin), finishing with a layer of
pasta. Pour the rest of the
sauce over the top, sprinkle
with the rest of the grated
cheese and flakes of butter.
Bake at the top of the oven for
15–20 minutes until golden
brown. Serve with a green
salad. This makes a filling one-
course meal.

*Pasta e fagioli
alla maruzzara**

**Pasta and Beans in Tomato
Sauce**

Serves 4

*A simple dish combining two of
the staples of the Italian diet.
Excellent for vegetarians.*

100g/3½oz canned plum
   tomatoes
2 cloves garlic, skinned
olive oil
1 teaspoon crushed oregano
salt
2 (400g/14oz) cans cannellini
   beans
250g/8oz mixed pasta (*pasta
   mista*)

Liquidise or crush the
tomatoes. Cut the garlic cloves
into 3 to 4 pieces. Coat the
base of a thick-bottomed
saucepan with olive oil and fry
the garlic until golden. Add the
tomatoes, oregano and salt to
taste, then cook for 5–6
minutes. Drain the beans, mix
them with the tomato sauce,
adding a glass of water, and
heat through.
Meanwhile, cook the pasta in a
pan of boiling salted water
until *al dente*. Drain and mix
with the beans and tomato
sauce. Serve in warmed
individual terracotta dishes.

RECIPES

*Penne all'arrabbiata**

'Furious' Quills

Serves 4

olive oil
2 cloves garlic, skinned
2 hot chillies, crushed
1 (400g/14oz) can plum
  tomatoes
salt
400g/14oz *penne* (pasta quills)
1 heaped tablespoon roughly
  chopped fresh parsley

Coat the base of a thick-bottomed frying pan with olive oil and fry the garlic and crushed chillies. Liquidise or crush the tomatoes. When the garlic is golden, add the tomatoes and salt to taste. Cook for 10–15 minutes until the sauce becomes thicker. Meanwhile, cook the pasta in a pan of boiling salted water until *al dente*. Drain well and mix with the sauce. Sprinkle generously with chopped parsley.

*Spaghetti aglio, olio, peperoncino**

Spaghetti with Oil, Garlic and Chilli

Serves 4

This simple but tasty dish, made in minutes, is a favourite with Italians late at night, after the cinema or even at the end of a wedding feast!

400g/14oz spaghetti
1 glass olive oil (about a wine
  glass, or more)
4 cloves garlic, skinned and
  finely chopped
1 dried red chilli, crushed
1 tablespoon roughly chopped
  fresh parsley (optional)

Cook the spaghetti in a pan of boiling salted water. Heat the oil in a small frying pan and add the garlic and chilli. Fry over a low heat so that the garlic becomes crunchy. When the spaghetti is *al dente*, drain well and mix with the oil and garlic. Serve immediately, sprinkled with chopped parsley, if using.

*Rigatoni alla pizzaiola**

Rigatoni, Pizza-maker Style

Serves 4

The meat is delicious served with chipped potatoes as a main course.

1½ (400g/14oz) cans plum
  tomatoes
3 cloves garlic, skinned
olive oil
1 teaspoon crushed oregano
4 slices lean beef (or 4 thin
  steaks)
salt
400g/14oz *rigatoni*
75g/3oz Parmesan cheese,
  grated, to serve

Liquidise or crush the tomatoes. Cut the garlic cloves into 3–4 pieces. Coat the base of a deep thick-bottomed frying pan with olive oil, add the tomatoes, garlic, oregano, beef and salt to taste. Simmer over a low heat, stirring occasionally, for about 30 minutes until the sauce becomes thicker and darker. Meanwhile, cook the *rigatoni* in a pan of salted water so that the pasta will be cooked *al dente* just as the sauce is ready. Drain well and mix with the sauce, leaving the meat for the main course. Serve with grated Parmesan cheese.

Trenette al pesto*

'Flattened' Spaghetti with Fresh Basil Paste

Serves 4

This is perhaps best made in your food processor at home, but it would be a shame not to try the 'chopped' version. The fresh Italian basil is too good to miss. Don't forget to take a packet of pine kernels home.

2 large bunches fresh basil
2–3 mint leaves (not necessary with Ligurian basil)
2 cloves garlic, skinned
1 tablespoon pine kernels
75g/3oz pecorino cheese, grated
about ⅔ wine glass olive oil
400g/14oz *trenette* or *linguine*

Wash and pat dry the basil leaves, discarding the stalks. Finely chop together the basil, mint, garlic and pine kernels either on a chopping board or in a food processor, adding part of the grated cheese as

Pesto is a classic Italian sauce

you chop. Transfer the chopped ingredients to a bowl and slowly beat in the oil and the rest of the cheese until a thick, creamy paste is obtained.
Meanwhile, cook the pasta in a pan of boiling salted water until *al dente*. Drain, keeping a cup of pasta water. Mix the pasta and pesto together, adding enough pasta water to make a creamy sauce which coats the pasta. Serve immediately.

RECENTS

*Risotto ai funghi porcini***

Mushroom Risotto

Serves 4

Packets of dried porcini *(edible boletus mushrooms) can be found in all Italian grocers and supermarkets.*

25g/1oz packet of dried
  porcini
olive oil
1 small onion, skinned and
  finely chopped
300g/10oz risotto rice
1 glass dry white wine
about 1 litre/2 pints boiling
  meat stock
knob of butter or margarine
75g/3oz Parmesan cheese,
  grated

Cover the *porcini* with a little boiling water and leave to soak for about 30 minutes, then squeeze out gently and roughly chop. Reserve a tablespoon of the liquid. Coat the base of a shallow saucepan with olive oil and fry the onion until transparent. Add the rice. As soon as it has absorbed the oil, add the wine. As soon as this has been absorbed, stirring all the time, start adding the boiling stock, just enough to cover the rice. Allow the rice to absorb it before adding more. When the rice is half cooked, add the *porcini* and reserved liquid. The risotto is ready when the rice is just cooked through and is neither too dry nor too liquid. Stir in the knob of butter and a third of the grated cheese. Allow to melt into the risotto before serving with the rest of the cheese, to be added as desired.

Good risotto is moist and creamy

Brasato al Barolo**

Braised Beef in Barolo Wine

Serves 6

750g/1lb 10oz lean beef
50g/2oz lean streaky bacon
1 medium onion, skinned and
  sliced
1 large carrot, peeled and
  sliced
1 stick celery, sliced
rosemary, 2 cloves, 1 clove
  garlic, 1 bay leaf and 2–3
  peppercorns tied in a muslin
  bag
1 bottle of Barolo wine
flour
50g/2oz butter
salt and pepper
small glass brandy
cornflour, if necessary

Lard the meat with half the
bacon. Finely chop the
remaining bacon. Put the meat
in a deep bowl with the onion,
carrot, celery and the herb
and spice bag. Pour the wine
over the meat, cover and leave
to marinate in a cool place
overnight.
Remove the meat, pat dry and
roll in flour. Melt the butter in a
flameproof casserole, fry the
chopped bacon and brown the
meat well on all sides. Pour in
the brandy and cook for a
minute or so. Add the
marinade. When it comes to
the boil, cook for 15 minutes
before removing the spices.
Season to taste, cover and
braise over a low heat for
2½–3 hours.
Remove the meat and keep
warm. Liquidise the sauce,
then bring it back to the boil
and thicken with a little
blended cornflour, if
necessary. Adjust for salt.
Thinly slice the meat and
serve, coated with the sauce,
on a warmed platter, with
potato purée or POLENTA.

Costoletta alla milanese*

Boneless Milanese Cutlets

Serves 4

*These golden fried cutlets are
similar to* Wiener Schnitzel.
*The butcher will flatten the
meat for you if you ask.*

2 small eggs (size 6)
salt
grated rind of ½ lemon
1 small packet toasted
  breadcrumbs
4 large thin slices lean veal or
  young beef
butter, margarine or olive oil,
  for frying
1 large lemon, cut into wedges

Break the eggs into a dish and
beat well, adding salt and the
lemon rind. Put a pile of
breadcrumbs on to a sheet of
greaseproof paper next to the
dish.
Remove any fat from the meat
and pound thinly with a meat-
mallet. Cut each slice in two.
Coat with egg and
breadcrumbs, pressing them
well on to the meat with the
palms of your hands. Fry until
golden. Serve piping hot with
the lemon wedges.

RECIPES

Saltimbocca alla romana

Roman 'Jump-in-the-mouths'

Serves 4

8 small thin slices veal
salt and pepper
8 small sage leaves
4 slices Parma ham, halved
butter or olive oil for frying
1 glass dry white wine

Trim the fat off the veal. Lightly season the slices and place a sage leaf on the centre of each. Top each slice of veal with half a slice of ham and secure with a wooden cocktail stick. Fry the slices in butter or olive oil over a high heat until cooked. Add the wine and continue cooking until the sauce becomes thick. Serve immediately, pouring the sauce over the escalopes.

*Fegato alla veneziana**

Venetian-style Liver

Serves 4

Venice's best known dish.

2 large onions, skinned
olive oil
600g/1¼lb calves' liver, sliced
salt and pepper
1 small glass dry white wine

Finely slice the onions lengthways. Coat the base of a thick-bottomed frying pan with olive oil, add the onions, cover and cook until transparent, stirring occasionally to prevent burning. Cut the liver into short, thin strips, season and add to the onions. Cook over a high heat, stirring all the time, until the liver is almost cooked. Add the wine and cook until the sauce becomes thick. Serve immediately with potato purée or POLENTA.

*Piselli al prosciutto**

Ham-flavoured Peas

Serves 4

These peas are also delicious mixed with pasta as a first course. Bacon can be used instead of Parma ham.

1 thick slice Parma ham, about
   100g/3½oz
olive oil
1 medium onion, skinned and
   finely chopped
450g/14½oz packet small
   frozen peas (petits pois)
salt

Chop the ham into small pieces. Coat the bottom of a wide saucepan or large frying pan with olive oil. Heat the oil, then fry the onion until transparent, adding the ham after about 5–7 minutes. Add the peas and stir in just enough water to cover. Add salt to taste and bring to the boil. Reduce the heat, if necessary, and simmer until the peas are tender, and most of the liquid has evaporated. Serve hot or warm.

A tasty choice for vegetarians

Melanzane alla parmigiana**

Aubergines, Parma Style

Serves 4

A filling one-course meal.

800g/1¾lb small, firm
  aubergines
coarse-grained cooking salt
olive oil
8–10 fresh basil leaves
500g/1lb mozzarella cheese
1 (400g/14oz) can plum
  tomatoes
salt and pepper
100g/3½oz Parmesan cheese,
  grated

Rinse, dry and cut the
aubergines lengthways into
slices about 0.25cm/⅛ inch
thick. Layer them in a
colander, sprinkling a little
cooking salt between each
layer. Place a weight (a deep
saucepan full of water is ideal)
on top and leave for about 1
hour for the salt to bring out
the bitter juices. Rinse the
aubergines under cold running
water and squeeze well.
Fry the slices in olive oil until
browned on each side. Drain
well on kitchen paper.
Set the oven at 200°C, 400°F,
gas 6. Tear the basil leaves
into small pieces. Cut the
mozzarella into thin slices.
Liquidise or crush the
tomatoes, seasoning them
slightly. Spread a little of the
tomatoes over the base of an
ovenproof dish. Cover with a
layer of aubergines, followed
by a little more tomato, a few
torn basil leaves, half the
mozzarella and sprinkle half
the grated Parmesan on top.
Repeat these layers, using up
all the ingredients. Bake in the
oven for about 30 minutes until
golden on top. Serve warm (not
too hot) or cold.

RECIPES

Frittata di zucchini *

Courgette 'Omelette'

Serves 4

4 large eggs (size 1)
50g/2oz Parmesan cheese, grated
salt and pepper
olive oil
1 medium onion, skinned and finely chopped
6 smallish courgettes, thinly sliced

Beat the eggs with the cheese, salt and pepper. Heat a little olive oil in a large non-stick frying pan and fry the onion. Add the courgettes and cook until just tender.
Cover the vegetables with the egg mixture and cook over a low heat, without stirring, until set and golden underneath. Slide the omelette on to a large plate, turn the frying pan upside down and place it over the *frittata*. Holding the plate carefully, rapidly turn the frying pan over and cook the *frittata* on the other side. Serve hot or cold.

Italian-style omelette

Mozzarella in carrozza *

'Mozzarella in Coaches'

Serves 4

The bread is best if not fresh. Make sure the slices are not too dissimilar from the size of the mozzarella slices.

2 large eggs (size 1)
salt and pepper
8 small thin slices bread
4 slices mozzarella cheese about 1cm/½inch thick
olive oil

Beat the eggs and salt and pepper to taste in a shallow bowl. Remove the bread crusts and make 'sandwiches' with the mozzarella. Dip them in the beaten egg, making sure that the bread is soaked with egg. Fry in olive oil until crisp and golden on both sides. Drain well on kitchen paper and serve piping hot.

*Pizzelle***

Small, Fried Pizzas

Serves 6

These are a real treat for the children as they are eaten in the fingers. Without the sauce, sprinkled with sugar and cinnamon, they also make a good dessert.

40g/1½oz fresh yeast
550ml/18fl oz tepid water
  (about 3 glasses)
700g/1½lb plain flour
1 teaspoon salt
1 (800g/1lb12oz) can plum
  tomatoes
3 large cloves garlic, skinned
8–10 fresh basil leaves
olive oil
salt
oil for deep frying
100g/3¾oz Parmesan cheese,
  grated, to serve

Dissolve the yeast in a little of the tepid water. Sift the flour and salt into a large bowl, making a well in the centre. Add the yeast and all the water. Mix together to form a soft, sticky dough. Turn out on to a well floured surface and knead for about 10 minutes, adding more flour if necessary, until the dough becomes soft and elastic. Shape into a long thin roll and cut into 24 pieces. Roll each piece into a small ball and put them on to a floured board. Cover and leave in a warm place to rise for about 1 hour. Meanwhile, prepare the sauce. Liquidise or crush the tomatoes. Cut the garlic cloves into 3–4 pieces. Tear the basil leaves into small pieces. Coat the base of a thick-bottomed frying pan with olive oil and fry the garlic until golden. Add the tomatoes, half the basil leaves and salt to taste. Cook for about 15 minutes until the sauce becomes thicker. Turn off the heat and add the rest of the basil.
When the *pizzelle* have doubled in size, flatten them into rounds, pulling them into shape with your fingers. Deep fry them, two or three at a time, depending on the size of the pan, until they float and are golden. Stack them on a serving plate, keeping them warm, and serve topped with the tomato sauce and grated Parmesan cheese.

*Insalata caprese**

Capri Salad

Serves 4

4 large tomatoes
800g/1¾lb mozzarella cheese
10–12 fresh basil leaves
olive oil
salt and pepper

Thinly slice the tomatoes. Cut the mozzarella into slices, about 1cm/½inch thick. Arrange them both on a serving platter. Tear the basil leaves into small pieces and use to garnish the tomatoes and mozzarella. Sprinkle with olive oil and serve immediately, everyone seasoning their own portion.

RECIPES

*Panzanella**

Serves 4

This refreshing snack is sometimes eaten for breakfast in the summer, in the south.

6 large ripe tomatoes
salt
8–10 fresh basil leaves
4 *freselle* (large ring-shaped rusks)
1 small red-skinned onion, skinned and thinly sliced
olive oil

Roughly chop the tomatoes, adding salt to taste. Tear the basil leaves into small pieces. Dip the rusks in cold water, then place on individual plates. Top them with the tomatoes and onion, sprinkle generously with olive oil and basil. Eat while still crunchy, or allow to soak a little in the juices if preferred.

*Peperoni arrostiti**

Roasted Pepper Salad

Serves 4

3 large red or yellow peppers
1 tablespoon olive oil
salt
2 cloves garlic, skinned and chopped
1½ teaspoons crushed oregano

Wash and dry the peppers, leaving them whole, and place them on a sheet of foil under the grill. Cook, turning them over frequently, until the skin has charred and come away from the flesh. Allow to cool a little (but not become cold) before skinning them with your fingers. Remove the stalks and seeds, then tear the flesh lengthways into thin strips. Dress the pepper strips with oil, salt, garlic and oregano. Combine well and leave to cool before serving.

*Tonno e fagioli**

Tuna and Beans

Serves 6

A favourite starter in Italian restaurants abroad, this is substantial enough to serve for a light lunch.

1 red-skinned onion, skinned and thinly sliced
2 (400g/14oz) cans cannellini beans
2 (160g/5oz) cans tuna, flaked
olive oil
salt and pepper
juice of 1 lemon
1 tablespoon fresh parsley, roughly chopped

Leave the onion to soak a while in cold water. Drain the beans and empty them into a serving bowl. Add the skinned onion and tuna, then dress with olive oil, salt to taste and sprinkle generously with pepper. Add the lemon juice and mix lightly, taking care not to break the beans. Serve chilled, sprinkled with parsley and accompanied by chunks of crusty bread.

Insalata di riso*

Rice Salad

Serves 4–6

You can vary the ingredients to your liking in this tasty dish. It makes a refreshing change from sandwiches for picnics.

400g/14oz long-grain rice
100g/3½oz mild cheese
10 black olives
2 small frankfurters (*wurstel*)
6 medium gherkins
2 large tomatoes
2 hard-boiled eggs
1 (160g/5oz) can tuna, drained
  and flaked
juice of 1 large lemon
2 tablespoons olive oil
salt and pepper

Cook the rice in a pan of boiling water until *al dente*. Drain well and chill in the refrigerator. Dice the cheese, stone and roughly chop the olives, cut the frankfurters and gherkins into thin slices and roughly chop the tomatoes and hard-boiled eggs. Put all the ingredients, with the tuna, into a large bowl and add the rice and lemon juice. Mix well, adding the oil, and season to taste. Chill before serving.

Pesche al vino*

Peaches in Wine

Serves 4

6 large peaches
1½ tablespoons caster sugar
dry white or red wine

Skin, stone and cut the peaches into thin slices. Place them in a serving dish and add the sugar. Cover with wine and leave to marinate in the refrigerator, preferably for several hours. Serve chilled.

Rice salad, a variable feast

RECIPES

Zabaione al Marsala **

Marsala-flavoured Egg Flip

Serves 4

Cream sherry makes a good substitute for Marsala.

4 egg yolks
4 tablespoons caster sugar
8 egg shells of Marsala wine
sponge fingers for dipping

Whisk the egg yolks and sugar in a bowl until thick, foamy and pale. Place the bowl over a pan of boiling water and, while still whisking, slowly add the Marsala, a shellful at a time. Continue whisking until the mixture is thick, light and creamy. **Never** let the mixture boil or it will curdle. Serve hot or cold in long-stemmed wine glasses with sponge fingers for dipping.

Zabaione, a popular dessert

Tiramisù **

Pick-me-up

Serves 6

Double cream can be substituted for the mascarpone.

3 eggs, separated
300g/10oz caster sugar
300g/10oz *mascarpone*
1 small glass brandy
200g/7oz sponge fingers
   (*savoiardi*)
1 teacup strong black coffee,
   slightly sweetened
1 tablespoon cocoa powder

Whisk the egg yolks with the sugar in a bowl until thick, pale and creamy. Add the *mascarpone* and brandy and continue whisking until well mixed. Whisk the egg whites until they form stiff peaks and gently fold them into the mixture.

In a shallow serving dish, layer the creamy mixture with the sponge fingers quickly dipped in coffee, finishing with a layer of creamy mixture. Chill in the refrigerator for several hours. Serve thickly dredged with cocoa.

SPECIAL EVENTS

Christmas

Italians tend to spend Christmas with the family, starting with an enormous dinner on Christmas Eve finishing just in time for everyone to go to Midnight Mass. The menu is traditionally based on fish and vegetable dishes followed by an incredible selection of fresh fruit, nuts, dried fruits and the traditional Christmas cakes, PANETTONE or PANDORO, not to mention all the regional Christmas specialities. A typical menu could be: seafood salad, spaghetti with clam sauce, baked sea bass, fried squid and prawns, broccoli, mixed salad, fresh fruit/nuts/dried fruit, STRUFFOLI/PANETTONE. Lunch on Christmas day is served later than usual, starting with stuffed pasta in consommé followed by a roast (often turkey nowadays), potatoes, vegetables and, once again, a selection of fruit, nuts and cakes.

New Year

New Year's Eve means another enormous dinner, this time lasting through into the New Year. In the home it is often fish based but the restaurants really go to town inventing the most incredible menus comprising starters, two or three first courses, fish, meat, game, vegetables, fruit, dessert and, after midnight, sliced, boiled sausage with lentils to guarantee wealth in the coming year!

Carnevale

Not to be confused with carnivals, *carnevale* is the period before Lent, from the Thursday up until the Tuesday before Ash Wednesday. Cakes such as CHIACCHIERE, FRAPPE and CASTAGNOLE are traditionally served at the various fancy dress parties which take place during *carnevale* time. Some regions also have special rich dishes, such as LASAGNE ALLA NAPOLETANA which is a much enjoyed treat before the privations of Lent.

Easter

Chocolate Easter eggs of all sizes, from the tiny filled ones sold by the *etto* (100g/4oz) to the gigantic ones raffled off in bars, appear all over Italy soon after *carnevale*. They all have a 'surprise' hidden in the centre, which can be anything from a plastic monster to good quality costume jewellery, depending on the price. Easter Sunday lunch traditionally starts with salami and hard-boiled eggs, followed by freshly made stuffed pasta in a sauce or consommé and roast lamb or goat. The COLOMBA is a special Easter cake found everywhere, along with regional specialities such as PIZZA DI PASQUA from Umbria, TORTA PASQUALINA from Liguria and PASTIERA NAPOLETANA.

Festa Days

Feste are religious celebrations. Some *festa* days have special cakes, such as BIGNÉ DI SAN GIUSEPPE on St Joseph's day. Look out for

A Florentine café

regional saints' days. Villages and towns always have a fair with street stalls selling regional specialities, toasted nuts, olives and candy floss to celebrate their patron saint.

Sagre

Look out for the local *Sagra del...*, a festival to celebrate the harvesting of certain fruit and vegetables, or the making of wine or sausages. They often take place at weekends and the whole village takes part in the making and selling of local dishes and products made from the foodstuff in question. Grapes, artichokes, wine, truffles, chestnuts, cherries and sausages are just a few examples.

EATING OUT

There is a vast selection of places where you can eat out in Italy with somewhere to suit everybody's pocket and taste, from take-away pizza shops to top-class restaurants. Italians eat out frequently; some even start their day by breakfasting with a CAPPUCCINO and CORNETTO in the bar. This is followed by mid-morning coffee, with or without an accompanying snack, and lunch in the local *trattoria* around 13.00 or 13.30 hours, unless it is possible to get home. Some, however, prefer to return to the bar for a sandwich or to buy a slice of pizza from the nearest shop, as most office workers have only an hour for lunch. Mid-afternoon usually means another visit to the bar for a quick coffee before going home, when they may stop on the way at the *tavola calda* (take-away) or *friggitoria* (fried food shop) to pick up something for supper. Eating out for pleasure usually takes place in the evenings, except on Sundays, when lunch in a characteristic restaurant in the country is very common. The evening eating places range from the cheaper, less pretentious *trattoria*, *pizzeria* or *birreria* to the elegant, carpeted restaurants with their soft music and, very often, expensive menus. As a general rule, fish dishes are more expensive than meat, especially if you let yourself be tempted by the roast fish and seafood! Whatever the type of restaurant, however, VAT has always been included in the prices quoted, and the bill, usually brought only when asked for, will include cover charge (which includes bread) and service. Tipping in the region of 10 per cent is expected – unless, of course, you have been served badly. Eating places always seem to be full, whatever day of the week it is. So if you are not an early eater, it is wise to book a table, especially on Saturday evenings, unless you don't mind waiting. Every bar or eating place closes on a fixed day every week and should display a notice saying which day this is: *Chiusura settimanale – lunedi* (Closing day – Monday). At holiday times, this may be waived.

SNACK BAR
Bar
Bars can be found on all street corners and are part of Italian everyday life. They are places where people meet, argue, fall out, make up, put the world to rights, or simply buy the family milk. They open early in the morning at 06.00 or 06.30 hours and close in the evening any time between 21.00 hours and midnight; some even stay open until the early hours of the morning. They serve coffee and drinks of all kinds both soft and alcoholic. In the mornings, they sell freshly baked sweet rolls of all shapes and sizes, the most common being the CORNETTO, which is similar to the French croissant. During the morning they start

preparing sandwiches and rolls for lunch and often serve slices of pizza, hot dogs and hamburgers, too. Most bars have tables outside. They should all display a price list clearly indicating the difference between the prices you pay standing at the counter and those with waiter service at a table, which is more expensive – sometimes more than double. Pay at the cash till before ordering at the counter, unless you prefer to sit at a table. Hand in the receipt at the counter to get your order.

At the Cash Till:
Two coffees and two *cornetti*, please.
Due cappuccini e due cornetti, per favore.
doo-e cap-poot-chEE-ni eh doo-e cor-nEt-ti pair fa-vO-re
Here's your receipt!
Ecco lo scontrino!
Ec-co lo scon-trEE-no.
Your receipt?
Lo scontrino?
lo scon-trEE-no
Here it is
Eccolo!
Ec-co-lo
May we sit down?
Possiamo sederci?
pos-siA-mo se-dEr-chi
May I sit down?
Posso sedermi?
pOs-so se-dEr-mi

PIZZA SHOPS
Pizza a Taglio/Pizza Rustica
These pizza shops sell pizza by the 'metre'. It is made on large trays, topped with all kinds of different foods and baked in special electric ovens. It is cut

into slices depending on how much you want, weighed and wrapped in paper. It can be eaten on the premises (most shops provide a few stools and cans of beer or soft drinks), consumed walking down the street, or taken home. Many shops of this kind also make savoury rice balls (SUPPLÌ), potato or chicken croquettes, cheese dreams (*mozzarella in carrozza*) and barbecued chickens.

TAKE-AWAYS
Rosticceria/Tavola Calda
These take-aways are sometimes attached to a bar, but they also exist in their own right. They are similar to self-service restaurants where you ask for portions of the food displayed in the glass-fronted counters, then either eat it at one of the tables provided or have it wrapped to take away. They sell pasta or rice dishes, a choice of main courses and vegetables and usually offer a selection of cheese and fruit, too. Bottles of wine, beer and soft drinks are also on sale. They are a favourite place for lunch or a quick snack before going to the cinema or theatre.

FRIED FOOD SHOP
Friggitoria
As their name suggests, these shops specialise in fried food and are mainly found in the south of Italy. Here, you can buy small pizzas topped with tomato sauce (PIZZELLE), savoury doughnuts flavoured with ham, cheese or anchovy fillets, sliced vegetables dipped in batter, prawns and

rings of squid, potato croquettes and many more delicacies – as long as they are fried. Like the pizza shops, they provide a few stools to enable you to enjoy your snack piping hot or, if you prefer, you can have it wrapped to take away.

LOCAL BARS
Bottiglieria/Cantina/ Fiaschetteria/Trani
The original 'bottle shops' or 'flask shops' are types of very basic eating places with plain formica-topped tables and bare painted walls. Here the local senior citizens (all male) go to pass the time by playing cards, chatting and drinking the local wine, which is served in the quarter (*quartino*), half (*mezzo*) and litre measures with their characteristic seal. They sometimes serve a simple meal such as cured ham, cheese and olives but you usually have to provide your own food. For example take your own sandwiches, some ham or other snack. The name *bottiglieria* or *fiaschetteria* can sometimes be misleading, however, as nowadays some of them have been turned into ordinary *trattorie*.

ROMAN-STYLE RESTAURANTS
Cucina/Osteria/Hostaria
Some of these traditional Roman-style restaurants can be very characterful, housed in an old wine cellar with a vaulted ceiling. Others are spartan and simple, with wooden chairs and tables in a plain, white-washed room with

a glass frontage separating it from the street. Whatever the setting, however, the food is usually deliciously home-made and wholesome. Prices are kept to a minimum as the tablecloths are often sheets of paper and the business is usually family-run, with sons and daughters serving at table, mother in the kitchen and father overseeing it all. This type of restaurant is usually busier at lunchtime, serving lunch to the local workmen, than in the evenings, when they tend to close earlier than other eating establishments.

PIZZA PARLOUR
Pizzeria
Pizza restaurants are usually open only in the evenings, except for a few in large cities which are open at lunchtime to cater for office workers and tourists. Pizza, however, is traditionally eaten in the

Cafés and bars are places for meeting as well as eating

evening and the *pizzerie* are packed with entire families, groups of young friends or couples fitting in a quick pizza before or after the cinema. They usually open at around 19.00 hours and close around midnight (earlier in the north). Apart from pizzas and stuffed pizzas (CALZONI), they will serve savoury toasts (CROSTINI), rice balls (SUPPLÌ), potato croquettes (CROCCHETTE DI PATATE) and, on Fridays, fried fillets of cod (*filetti di baccalà*). They also usually provide other 'fillers' such as vegetables, cheese and fruit. Local wine is sold by the litre, but many Italians prefer beer with their pizza and the young drink Coke or orangeade. Some *pizzerie* are also *trattorie* and, therefore, offer a full menu.

EATING OUT

BEER-HOUSE
Birreria
These beer-houses are usually furnished in Tyrolean style, with trestle tables and benches carved in a light-coloured wood. They serve different types of draught and bottled beers, accompanied by typical south Tyrolean/Austrian dishes such as frankfurters with sauerkraut, smoked pork, goulash and mixed grills. They often serve pizza, too.

RESTAURANTS
Trattoria/Ristorante
Both names can be attributed to restaurants ranging from the more modest, cheaper ones to the extravagantly expensive ones which, by the way, are not always the best. *Trattoria* usually refers to the first category and *ristorante* to the second, but often the names are interchangeable, some *ristoranti* being very simple places while some so-called *trattorie* are very fashionable restaurants. You can usually judge from the menu on display outside what kind of prices you are letting yourselves in for. Both offer a full menu from starters through to the after-dinner coffee and liqueurs, which are sometimes 'on the house'. An aperitif is usually drunk at the nearby bar while waiting for a table. The meal begins with a starter (ANTIPASTO); many restaurants have a tempting display by the entrance to attract your attention on arrival. After the pasta, rice or soup course (*primo*) – of which you may ask for a half portion if you wish –

you then move on to the fish or meat (*secondo*), depending on the restaurant's speciality. Vegetables are nearly always served separately (and charged separately), unless otherwise stated. A choice of cheese, fresh fruit or a sweet completes the meal, which is accompanied by a bottle of wine or house wine served in a jug. If you do not like mineral water you can ask for a jug of tap water (*acqua semplice*). A basket of bread and bread sticks will always be brought to your table; you can ask for it to be refilled, as it is included in the cover charge.

Courses
Antipasto the first course or starter, consisting of a selection of dishes.
Primo The rice, pasta, or soup course of the meal.
Secondo The fish or meat dish.
Contorno Vegetables are served separately, after the fish or meat dish.
Dolce Fruit and cheese may complete the meal, or desserts may be offered in formal restaurants.

Many Italians, nowadays, skip the main course and simply have a starter and a plate of pasta or risotto followed by vegetables or salad, or they may choose a starter instead of the meat or fish dishes. It is usually the typical 'tourist' restaurant which still frowns upon not ordering a main course. Talking about tourist restaurants, it is usually a pity to order the so-called 'Tourist Menu' (*Menu Turistico*). Unless you are very lucky, it will avoid the regional specialities and include dishes such as spaghetti with plain tomato sauce, roast chicken, chipped potatoes and fruit. It is much more interesting to order from the menu where you can try out exciting new flavours and taste combinations.

Booking a Table:
Good morning. I'd like to book a table for four, this evening.

Buon giorno. Vorrei prenotare un tavolo per quattro, stasera.
Bwon jOr-no. vor-rEh-i pre-no-tA-re oon tA-vo-lo pair quAt-tro, sta-sE-ra

What time?

A che ora?
a keh Ora

At half past eight.

Alle otto e mezza.
al-le Ot-to eh mEd-dza

Very well. What's your name?

Va bene. Quale è il suo nome?
va bE-ne, quAh-le eh il sooh-o nO-me

At the Restaurant:
Good evening. How many?

Buona sera. Quante persone?
bwO-na sE-ra quAn-te pair-sO-ne

Good evening. There are four of us. (We've booked. The name's . . . .)

Buona sera. Siamo in quattro. (Abbiamo prenotato. Il nome è . . . .)
bwO-na sE-ra. siA-mo in

quAt-tro (ab-biA-mo pre-no-tA-to. il nO-me Eh. . . .)

Thank you. May I have the menu, please.

Grazie. Posso avere il menu, per favore?
grA-tsieh. POs-so a-vE-re il me-nOO pair fa-vO-re

Excuse me. What is this?
(*indicating something on menu*)

Mi scusi. Che cos'è questo?
mee scOO-zi. ke co-zeh quE-sto

That's . . . . . .

Quello è. . . . . .
qu-El-lo eh. . . . . .

Tempting displays help you choose

How's it cooked?

Com'è cucinato?

co-mEh coo-chi-nA-to

It's done with . . . . . .

E' fatto con . . . . . .

Eh fAt-to con

We'll decide afterwards, thank you.

Decideremo dopo, grazie.

de-chi-de-rE-mo dO-po, grA-tsieh

Anything to drink?

Da bere?

da bEh-re

A bottle of mineral water and some house wine.

Una bottiglia di acqua minerale e vino della casa.

OO-na bot-tEE-lya di Acqua mi-ne-rAle eh vEE-no del-la cA-sa

Red or white?

Rosso o bianco?

rOs-so o biAn-co

White, thank you.

Bianco, grazie.

biAn-co, grA-tsieh

It was/They were very good.

Era buonissimo/
Erano buonissimi.

*Era bwo-nEEs-si-mo/
E-ra-no bwo-nEEs-si-mi*

Waiter! The bill, please.

Cameriere! Il conto, per favore.

ca-me-riEh-re il cOn-to pair fa-vO-re

Here you are!

Eccolo!

Ec-co-lo

Here you are. Keep the change.

Ecco a Lei. Tenga il resto!

Ec-co a LEh-i. tEn-ga il rE-sto

Have you any . . . . . please?

Avete del . . . . . per favore?

a-vE-te del . . . . . pair fa-vO-re

A half portion, please.

Una mezza porzione, per favore.

OOna mEd-dza por-tsiO-ne, pair fa-vO-re

I'm a vegetarian.

Sono vegetariano.

sO-no ve-je-ta-riA-no

Is there any meat in it?

C'è della carne dentro?

chEh del-la cAr-ne dEn-tro

very/too

molto/troppo

mOl-to/trOp-po

cold/hot

freddo/caldo

frEd-do/cAl-do

cooked/raw/burnt

cotto/crudo/bruciato

*cOt-to/crOO-do/
broo-chA-to*

with/without/only

con/senza/soltanto

con/sEn-tsa/sol-tAn-to

ICE-CREAM PARLOUR
Gelateria

Why not stop after the vegetable course at the restaurant and move on to a *gelateria* (ice-cream parlour) for dessert? Here you can buy ice-creams in every flavour you can think of. They are either served in cones or small cardboard cartons for eating in the street, or in silver sundae dishes or glasses topped with a mountain of freshly whipped cream to be enjoyed while sitting at a table, with waiter service. You can also buy ice-cream by the kilo, to be taken away in special polystyrene boxes to keep it from melting. The shops stay open from late morning through to late evening, especially in the summer.

CHILDREN

Children enjoy pizzeria meals

As a general rule, Italians adore babies and children and tend to spoil them dreadfully. Often the magic word *bambino* will miraculously open doors, obtain favours and persuade even the most grumpy waiter to smile. Babies' bottles are heated up in bars without any problem, and baby foods can be found in all chemists (*farmacia*), grocers and supermarkets. There may not be as much choice as in Britain because Italians, as in all their cooking, prefer not to use ready-made foods unless absolutely necessary.

There is no age restriction in bars, and glasses of water are given freely if one of the party has ordered something. Restaurants will often produce a high-chair and can always be counted on to make *pastina in brodo* (small pasta shapes in soup) even when it is not on the menu. When sprinkled with grated cheese, this makes a filling meal, especially when followed by a slice of grilled meat or fish and fresh fruit. Half portions of most dishes can be ordered but the waiter will cheerfully bring an extra plate if you prefer to share your adult portions, although a cover charge will probably appear on the bill. *Pizzerie* are, of course, the children's favourite where they can pick the pizza up in their fingers and no-one will say anything! Eating outside is also a boon to parents as the children, once finished, can play (if it is safe and within reason) near by.

For the baby/little boy.
For the baby/little girl.
> Per il bambino.
> Per la bambina.
> *pair il bam-bEE-no/*
> *pair la bam-bEE-na*

Please, could you warm up the baby's bottle?

> Per favore, può riscaldare il biberon?
> *pair fa-vO-re, pwO ris-cal-dA-re il bi-be-rOn*

May I have a glass of water?

> Posso avere un bicchiere d'acqua?
> *pos-so av-Eh-re oon bic-kiE-re dAc-qua*

Have you got a high-chair, please?

> Avete un seggiolone, per favore?
> *avEh-te oon sed-jo-lO-ne, pair fa-vO-re*

A half-portion of . . . ., please.

> Mezza porzione di . . . ., per favore.
> *med-dza por-tsiO-ne di . . . . pair fa-vO-re*

May I have a plate/spoon/teaspoon?

> Posso avere un piatto/cucchiaio/cucchiaino?
> *pos-so avE-re oon piAt-to/cooc-kyA-yo/cooc-kya-EEno*

Without dressing/oil.

> Senza condimento/olio.
> *sEn-tsa con-di-mEn-to/O-lio*

SPECIAL DIETS

Vegetarians, even vegans, will have no difficulty in finding sufficient variety of dishes to suit their needs. Even the most basic restaurant can offer *spaghetti al pomodoro* (spaghetti in tomato sauce) followed by some kind of substantial vegetable dish such as baked aubergines (sometimes with cheese), artichokes, peppers, green vegetables or salad. Bean dishes are common, but watch out for the ham used to flavour some regional recipes.

To avoid fried foods, order fish and meat *alla griglia* (grilled) and, if you prefer, ask for it to be cooked without oil *'senza olio, per favore'*. Boiled vegetables served with oil and lemon (*all'agro*) can always be found and fresh fruit is served in all restaurants as dessert. Wholemeal breadsticks and bread are beginning to appear in some more fashionable restaurants and bars but are not very common.

Wholemeal pasta, although readily available in shops and supermarkets, is not usually served except in vegetarian restaurants in large cities.

TIGHT BUDGET

Self Catering

Buy a good supply of dried and canned foods from the nearest supermarket, as these can cost quite a bit more in the village stores or local grocer's shop. Markets are best for freshness and cheapness when buying fruit and vegetables, although roadside stalls can also offer 'bargains' if you are buying in large quantities. Fish can be picked up cheaply in the markets at closing time, if you are prepared to take whatever is left. It is often sold off at as little as half price. (Remember that white fish is twice as expensive as meat, but oily fish such as anchovies and mackerel are much cheaper.) Bottles of wine and liqueurs are, again, usually cheaper at supermarkets but, of course, some special locally made wines and liqueurs are only available at source.

Eating Out

The cheapest eating place is often the unpretentious *trattoria* on the corner where you can get a full, wholesome meal quite inexpensively if you do not mind not having much choice. The *pizza a taglio* shops provide slices of pizza for economical, filling snacks, while in the *tavola calda/rosticceria* you can choose just a salad, if that is all you want. When eating out in restaurants, *pizzerie* and *trattorie*, always check the menu on display before entering, to see what kind of prices you are letting yourself in for!

PRACTICAL TIPS

Self Catering

Most self-catering apartments are well equipped with modern cookers and refrigerators, and they will have saucepans, coffee percolators, cutlery, plates and glasses. Disposable plastic plates and cups can be bought in packs of 50s or 100s, however, in most shops and supermarkets. They are well worth the small, extra cost! The water is drinkable, unless there has been some local disaster, and can safely be used for making ice-cubes.

Tummy Upsets

Boiled rice mixed with a little olive oil and grated Parmesan cheese is a favourite with Italians when not feeling too

well. Squeezed lemon juice is also excellent for stopping diarrhoea. When having to eat out, ask to eat *in bianco* (without sauces/plain) with everything grilled, poached or boiled.

Laws/Regulations

By law you should always make sure that you are given an official fiscal receipt (*ricevuta fiscale*) in restaurants, in case of spot checks by the Finance Police. The same applies to the receipt from the cash till in shops and bars. However, common practice is not always as strict with regard to providing receipts.

Cooling off with an ice-cream

LANGUAGE

LANGUAGE

Useful Phrases

Good morning Buongiorno
bwon-jOr-no
Good afternoon/evening
Buonasera
bwo-na-sEh-ra
Good night Buonanotte
bwo-na nOt-te
Hello/goodbye Ciao *chow*
Yes/No Si/No
see/no
I don't know
Non lo so
non lo sO
I'm sorry Mi dispiace
mee dis-piA-che
Excuse me . . . . Mi scusi . . . .
mee scOO-zi
Is there a toilet?
C'è un bagno?
chEh oon bA-nyo
Where is the telephone?
Dov'è il telefono?
do-vEh il te-lE-fo-no
Will you give me a telephone token, please?
Mi da un gettone, per favore?
mee dAh oon jet-tOne pair fa-vO-re
Can you repeat that, please?
Può ripetere per favore?
pwO ri-pE-te-re pair fa-vO-re
I haven't understood.
Non ho capito.
non oh ca-pEE-to
What is/your name?
Come si chiama?
cO-me si kiA-ma
What's the time?
Che ora è?
kEh Ora Eh
It's 6 o'clock
Sono le sei.
sO-no-le sEh-i

Breakfast/lunch/supper
Colazione/pranzo/cena
co-la-tsiO-ne/prAn-tso/chE-na

Days of the Week

Sunday domenica *do-mE-ni-ka*
Monday lunedì *loo-ne-dEE*
Tuesday martedì *mar-te-dEE*
Wednesday mercoledì
mer-co-le-dEE
Thursday giovedì *jo-ve-dEE*
Friday venerdì *ve-ner-dEE*
Saturday sabato *sA-ba-to*

Quantities

1 uno *OO-no*
2 due *dOOe*
3 tre *trEh*
4 quattro *quAt-tro*
5 cinque *chIn-que*
6 sei *sEh-i*
7 sette *sEt-te*
8 otto *Ot-to*
9 nove *nO-ve*
10 dieci *dyEh-chee*
11 undici *OOn-di-chee*
12 dodici *dO-di-chee*
13 tredici *trE-di-chee*
14 quattordici *quat-tOr-di-chee*
15 quindici *quIn-di-chee*
16 sedici *sEh-di-chee*
17 diciassette *dee-cha-sEt-te*
18 diciotto *dee-chOt-to*
19 diciannove *dee-cha-nO-ve*
20 venti *vEn-ti*
21 ventuno *ven-tOO-no*
22 ventidue *ven-ti-dOOe*
30 trenta *tr-En-ta*
40 quaranta *qua-rAn-ta*
50 cinquanta *chin-quAn-ta*
60 sessanta *ses-sAn-ta*
70 settanta *set-tAn-ta*
80 ottanta *ot-tAn-ta*
90 novanta *nov-An-ta*
100 cento *chen-to*
200 duecento *dooe-chEn-to*
1000 mille *mEEl-le*
2000 duemila *dooe mEE-la*

Weight and Volume

1 kg (kilo) Un chilo
oon kEE-lo
2 kg Due chili *dooe kEE-li*
100 g Cento grammi
chEn-to grAm-mi/
Un etto *oon Et-to*
200 g (grams) Due etti
dooe Et-ti
500 g Mezzo chilo
mEd-dzo kEE-lo
1 litre Un litro *oon lEE-tro*
¾ trequarti *tre-quAr-ti*
½ mezzo *mEd-dzo*
¼ un quarto *oon quAr-to*
a portion of una porzione di
oona por-tsiO-ne di
½ portion of mezza porzione
med-dza por-tsiO-ne di
a glass of un bicchiere di
oon bic-kiE-re di
a cup of una tazza di
oona tAt-tsa di
a slice of una fettina di
oona fet-tEE-na di
a piece of un pezzo di

Reading the menu is not too hard

oon pEt-tso di
a fillet of un filetto di
oon fi-lEt-to di

Hints on How to Pronounce Italian

1 Pronounce *every* letter, whatever its position in the word, eg Minestron<u>e</u>.

2 Accentuating the correct syllable is very important in Italian. To help you, stressed vowels are in capitals in the imitated pronunciation.
eg vino bianco (*vEE-no biAn-co*).

3 Italian 'a' is pronounced like 'a' in 'father', but shorter (not as in 'hat' or 'hate')
eg p<u>a</u>sta

4 Italian 'e' is pronounced like 'e' in best or 'a' in 'Mary' (not as in 'he')
eg b<u>e</u>n<u>e</u>

5 Italian 'i' is pronounced like 'ee' in 'sheep', but shorter (not as in 'right').
eg p<u>i</u>zza (*pEEt-tsa*)

6 Italian 'o' is pronounced like 'o' in 'pot' (not as in 'post')
eg mo<u>lt</u>o

7 Italian 'r' is always strongly pronounced – children imitating an electric buzzer with the tip of their tongue come close, eg buon gio<u>r</u>no

8 Double consonants in Italian are pronounced by lingering on the first of the two consonants
eg mamma (*mAm-ma*).

CONVERSION TABLES

NOTES ON USING THE RECIPES

Weights and measures are written in metric and imperial. Follow only one set of measures as they are not interchangeable.

Abbreviations
Metric
g–gram or gramme
kg–kilogram
ml–millilitre
Imperial
oz–ounce
lb–pound
fl oz–fluid oz

Metric/Imperial Weight Conversions

50g/2oz	350g/12oz
75g/3oz	500g/1lb
100g/4oz	700g/1½lb
150g/5oz	1kg/2lb
175g/6oz	1.5kg/3lb
250g/8oz	2kg/4lb

Metric/Imperial Fluid Conversions
125ml/4fl oz
150ml/¼ pint (5fl oz)
175ml/6fl oz
200ml/7fl oz
300ml/½ pint (10fl oz)
500ml/18fl oz
600ml/1 pint (20fl oz)
750ml/1¼ pints
1 litre/1¾ pints
2 litres/3½ pints

Spoon Measures
Spoon measures refer to the standard measuring spoons and all quantities are level unless otherwise stated. **Do not** use table cutlery and serving spoons instead of measuring spoons as their capacity varies.
½ teaspoon – 2.5ml
1 teaspoon – 5ml
1 tablespoon – 15ml (3 teaspoons)

Oven Temperatures
The following settings are used in the recipes providing centigrade, Fahrenheit and gas settings. However, cooking facilities in holiday accommodation may be limited or oven settings may be different or unreliable, therefore watch dishes carefully when baking in unfamiliar appliances.
110°C, 225°F, gas ¼
120°C, 250°F, gas ½
140°C, 275°F, gas 1
150°C, 300°F, gas 2
160°C, 325°F, gas 3
180°C, 350°F, gas 4
190°C, 375°F, gas 5
200°C, 400°F, gas 6
220°C, 425°F, gas 7
230°C, 450°F, gas 8
240°C, 475°F, gas 9

American Measures and Terms
Liquids: Imperial/American
8fl oz – 1 cup
16fl oz – 2 cups
20fl oz (1 pint) – 1 pint or 2½ cups
¼ pint – ⅔ cup
½ pint – ½ pint
Solids
Whole pounds and fractions of a pound are used for some ingredients such as butter, vegetables and meat. Cup measures are used for storecupboard foods, such as flour, sugar and rice. Butter is also measured by sticks.

Imperial/American
Butter – 8oz/1 cup (2 sticks)
Cheese, grated hard – 4oz/1 cup
Flour – 4oz/1 cup
Haricot beans, dried – 6oz/1 cup
Mushrooms, sliced – 8oz/2½ cups
Olives, whole – 4oz/1 cup
Parmesan cheese, grated – 1oz/3 tablespoons, 2oz/⅓ cup
Peas, shelled – 4oz/1 cup
Raisins – 6oz/1 cup
Rice (uncooked) – 8oz/1 cup

INDEX

Page numbers in italics
refer to recipes

The Automobile Association wishes to thank the following photographers for their assistance in the preparation of this book.

Eric Meacher was commissioned for photographs on pages 98, 100, 103, 104, 107, 108, 111, 112 and the cover picture.

Tony Souter was commissioned for the remaining pictures with the exception of pages 19, 28, 58, 68, 119, 125 (Peter Wilson) and pages 6, 79, 96, 114 (Barrie Smith).

Author's Acknowledgements
The author would like to thank her husband, Manlio Conte, for his invaluable collaboration on Italian wines, and the directors of the International House language schools around Italy for their help with regional specialities.